FOLK TALE PLAYS ROUND THE WORLD

A collection of royalty-free,
one-act plays about lands far and near

by
PAUL T. NOLAN

Publishers   PLAYS, INC.   Boston

Library of Congress Cataloging in Publication Data

Nolan, Paul T.
  Folk tale plays round the world.

  Includes selections from the author's Round-the-world plays for young people, published 1970.
  Summary: Sixteen one-act plays based on the folklore, customs, and national characteristics of various countries including China, Greece, Holland, Spain, and Poland.

  1. Children's plays, American. 2. One-act plays, American. [1. Plays] I. Title.
PS3564.o37F6   1982   812'.54   82-14188
ISBN 0-8238-0253-1   (pbk.)

MANUFACTURED IN THE UNITED STATES OF AMERICA

PREFACE

From earliest times, there have been storytellers who told folk tales to small groups in their villages or communities — stories that, of course, they had only heard, not read. In this way, they kept alive the oral tradition of storytelling and passed on the local lore from generation to generation.

Early in the 19th century, two remarkable young men, Jacob and Wilhelm Grimm, started to collect this previously unwritten form of literature, not only because it offered entertainment but because they found in it essential truths and wisdom, often more revealing than formal literature or historical events.

Every nation has its own folk literature — plays, poetry, folk tales — but because the themes and plots of these tales deal with universal human problems, it is not easy to distinguish those of one country from those of another, especially within Europe, the Latin American countries, the Far East, or Africa. Some tales center around natural disasters — famine, storms, earthquakes — which have evoked fear over the centuries. *The Double Nine of Chih,* one of the plays in this collection, is an example of this kind of folk tale. Others deal with historical events — great dramatic moments in the growth of a nation, the establishment of a new government, victory over an oppressor or invader — as in *Robin Hood and The Match in Nottingham, The Skill of Pericles,* and *The Son of William Tell.*

Because until relatively recent times most people lived in rural areas, many folk tales used animal characters endowed with human characteristics like speech, and wiliness that helps outwit an often superior or more powerful combatant, for instance, *Stanislaw and the Wolf.*

Most of the folk tales popular today have appeared in various forms in the folk literature of many nations, and in many different languages. *The Courters,* for example, exists in various versions in Italian, French, and English. The universal elements and themes in folk tales are not surprising, since the world

PREFACE

over, similar problems, fears, and hopes are common to all peoples. Fol
literature has an obvious kind of directness, dealing with types of peop
everyone knows: simple, good-natured, honest men and women, yes, an
villains, some of whom succeed despite great odds, because they are good c
clever or lucky, or a combination of these qualities. In spite of the fact that fol
tales often deal with the supernatural and with magic, they are generall
realistic.

In recent years, the popularity of folk tales has persisted and increased, eithe
in the traditional form or in new retellings. Isaac Bashevis Singer, for example
is one of the great tellers of folk tales, a talent which won him the Nobel Prize i
Literature.

The plays in this collection are dramatizations of a representative samplin
of some of the most popular folk tales representing various countries of th
world, legends, tales, clever anecdotes. Their continued durability and appe₂
result from the universality of their themes and believable human reactions
with which listeners and audiences readily identify.

PAUL T. NOLAN

Contents

JAPAN

MEXICO

NORWAY

POLAND

SCOTLAND

SPAIN

SWITZERLAND

UNITED STATES

THE DOUBLE NINE OF CHIH YUAN

(China)

As early as 2,000 B.C., the Chinese are believed to have had dramatic festivals, jugglers, sword dancers, and other forms of theatricals. By 1,000 B.C., the art of the shadow play had reached a degree of high perfection in China. These forms suggest that children must have been a part of the audience, and some of these forms are alive in Asia for children today. Traditional Chinese plays were very long, some running twelve hours; but it is to be supposed that spectators came and went at their leisure; at least that is now the custom of the Chinese theaters in San Francisco.

The Chinese stage is open. There are no curtains, but the place of the acting is indicated by a raised platform, with bamboo poles at both ends. The back stage has two doors, one for entrances and one for exits. And the stage is bare except for hand properties, brought on by the Property Man, an important person in the Chinese play. He is dressed in black or blue. He helps a character off with his coat before a strenuous piece of business that might soil it. He brings onstage a ladder representing the mountain over which the hero must laboriously climb. In this play, he narrates the action and also assists with the properties, although normally his role is simply that of stage hand.

The people of China have long lived off the soil, and since much of China is cold, winter is a time of great hardship. In stressing the need to prepare for the coming of winter, the Chinese invented a myth that dramatizes the killing effect of winter for those who are unprepared. "The Double Nine of Chih Yuan" is based upon this old Chinese legend. According to this tale, which goes back to 500 B.C., a wise man warned a friend that the killing frost was coming. The friend took his family and their belongings and fled to the mountains, to get above the frost. When they returned, they found the frost had killed everything that was left, but they were grateful for their escape. The arrival of the frost was the ninth day of the ninth month, so the Chinese people celebrated their escape on that date each year. They called the celebration the Double Nine, for the day and month. Some centuries later, kite flying became a part of the celebration, probably because the kite, too, flies above the frost. This play is a "mythical" explanation of how the kite became part of the Double Nine celebration.

The Double Nine Of Chih Yuan

Characters

THE PROPERTY MAN

HAN HSIN, *a wise, old man*

CHIH YUAN, *the father*

KUANYIN, *the mother*

YAO, *the son*

MIAO CHEN, *the daughter*

SETTING: *A bare stage.*

A picture of a snow-capped mountain hangs on rear wall. At left a door is marked "Entrance" and door at right is marked "Exit."

AT RISE: *A gong is hit and the* PROPERTY MAN *walks on stage from the right. He bows to the audience.*

PROPERTY MAN: This is a Chinese play, and I am the Property Man. It is my job to help the actors and to bring on the stage the objects they need. If you were Chinese, you would ignore me because I have no more part in this play than the American cameraman has in the movies made in Hollywood. But since you are not Chinese, I will explain. This stage is the farm of Chih Yuan, a poor but worthy farmer. And that mountain there is many miles from the farm of Chih Yuan, but during this play, he will have to climb it. Right now, the family of Chih Yuan are in the hut. When they come out, they will come through that door marked "Entrance." When they leave the stage, for any reason, no matter where they are going—into the house or to the pens to feed the goats—they will leave by that door, marked "Exit." Right now, Chih Yuan has a guest, the wise man, Han Hsin. Soon they will come out, and you will hear them. (*He bows.*) So with your kind permission, this humble servant takes his leave, and the play begins. (*Exit right, and the gong strikes again. Enter* Han Hsin *and* Chih Yuan *from "Entrance" Door.*)

Han Hsin: Even now while the sun's warm rays comfort these miserable, old bones, I smell it in the air. The killing frost.

Chih Yuan: You must be patient with me, Old Wise One. I am a simple farmer. In my whole life I have never been once to a city. I have never been once beyond the earth that I can see from my door. I have never seen a book, and you are the only man I have ever met who has been beyond the mountain. I am indeed a simple, ignorant man, a great fool.

Han Hsin: You are a simple man, Chih Yuan, it is true. But you are not ignorant, and you are no fool. You have used the earth about you well, and your family is a richer treasure than the pearls of the dragon. He who values the land and the life that lives on it is both wise and good.

Chih Yuan: And yet, now I must leave the land?

Han Hsin: Yes.

Chih Yuan: Why? When did I do evil to the earth? When did I take from it without returning to it? When did I allow the rains to cut gullies on the earth's face? Each year I have tilled the soil. I have saved the rain in time of plenty and fed it to the earth in time of want. What have I done wrong?

HAN HSIN: You have done no wrong. No man may rightly know what is beyond the mountain that he has never crossed. And no man rules the winds. From beyond the mountains comes the killing frost, carried by the wind. If you do not leave your land and take refuge in the caves of the mountains, you and all that live here will perish.

CHIH YUAN: Is there no other way?

HAN HSIN: Before winter comes the next time, you can prepare for it. Build stouter barns, lay in a supply of feed for the animals and wood for the fire. But now, it is too late. Your only escape lies in a flight to the mountains.

CHIH YUAN: I am indeed a fool.

HAN HSIN: No man is a fool who suffers once because he does not know. But when the ninth day of the ninth month comes again, if you have not learned, then you shall rightly call yourself a fool. Now you must make haste and prepare for your journey to the mountain.

CHIH YUAN: I am humbly grateful that you have come to me, Wise Old Man. I and my family would have died without you.

HAN HSIN: I shall accompany you on your journey and show you the way to live in the mountains.

CHIH YUAN: I am truly grateful.

HAN HSIN: But now call your family together. It is time for the preparation. (CHIH YUAN *goes to door marked "Exit" and calls.*)

CHIH YUAN: Wife! Your husband summons you and his

children to appear. (*He returns to center stage, and* KUANYIN, YAO, *and* MIAO CHEN *enter from door marked "Entrance." They go to the two men and stand silently before them with bowed heads.* YAO *carries a kite with him.* MIAO CHEN *carries a doll.*)

CHIH YUAN: Wife, it has been ordered that we must leave our home and journey to the mountains.

KUANYIN: Yes, my husband.

CHIH YUAN: You will prepare yourself and my children, taking only those things that we need for survival: warm clothing and food.

KUANYIN: Yes, my husband. And for how long shall I prepare?

CHIH YUAN: Until the killing frost has come and gone. Then we shall return to our home.

YAO: Honored Father, may I . . . ?

CHIH YUAN: My son, did I bid you speak?

YAO: The worthless son of an honored father humbly begs forgiveness.

CHIH YUAN: You may speak.

YAO: May worthless son carry his kite with him?

CHIH YUAN: (*Looking to* HAN HSIN) A kite is only a small thing.

HAN HSIN: Every ounce here will become a ton before we reach the caves of the mountains.

CHIH YUAN: No, my son. The kite must stay.

MIAO CHEN: Honored Father, may I take my doll?

CHIH YUAN: No, my daughter. Neither the kite nor the doll will suffer from the frost. Put them away for the spring. The doll must stay.

MIAO CHEN: Yes, Honored Father. I shall bid my doll sleep until I return.

YAO: You will want Chou to accompany us? Is it not so, Honored Father?

CHIH YUAN: Chou?

YAO (*Taking a small turtle from inside his shirt*): Our friend who carries his own house on his back.

CHIH YUAN: Such a small turtle. It would not feed us.

YAO: He is not food, Honored Father. He is a friend.

CHIH YUAN (*Looking at the turtle and then at* HAN HSIN): He *is* a small turtle.

HAN HSIN: A fly on your shoulder will become an elephant on your back before we reach the caves.

CHIH YUAN: No, my son, Chou must remain behind. The turtle must stay.

YAO: But will he not die of the killing frost, Father?

CHIH YUAN: Does my son question his father's wisdom?

YAO: Perhaps he will not die.

CHIH YUAN: Now, go and prepare. Wife, prepare the clothes and food. Daughter, latch the doors and put grass in the cracks. Son, prepare the animals for their journey. (*Bows to* HAN HSIN) And Wise Old Man, would you take rest in the lowly abode of Chih Yuan before beginning your journey?

HAN HSIN: I shall be most grateful. (CHIH YUAN *bows.* HAN HSIN *walks through the door marked "Exit," and* CHIH YUAN *follows him.*)

YAO: It is a hard thing to part with a friend.

KUANYIN: Does small son question the wisdom of his father?

YAO: I shall tend the animals, my mother.

KUANYIN: Small Son shall see that what is feared in the future can be faced if one lives bravely in the present. Come, Small Daughter, we have work to do.

MIAO CHEN: And I shall surround my doll with grass, too, so that the killing frost does not nip her nose and toes. (KUANYIN *and* MIAO CHEN *leave stage through door marked "Exit."*)

YAO: It is still a hard thing to leave a friend. (*Talks to turtle.*) Little Chou, it is too bad that you do not have wings. Then you could fly above the killing frost and hover near the great warm sun until I return. Yao will miss you, Little Friend. He will miss you when spring comes and we are again home. Who will watch me fly my kite if you are gone, Little Chou? (*He stops, looks at the turtle, then looks at his kite. He holds the turtle up in one hand, and he holds the kite in the other.*) It is true, you do not have wings, Little Chou. But you may fly. Our Honored Mother has said that the fearful future can be faced if we live bravely in the present. We shall live bravely, Little Chou. (*He exits through door marked "Exit."*)

PROPERTY MAN (*Comes on stage. He carries a small stepladder and an animal skin*): Now, while the small family of Chih Yuan prepare for their journey, I shall make the stage ready for you. (*Points to ladder, which he sets down in front of the painting of the mountain.*) This is the mountain which they must climb. The way is long and hard, and they must stop many times on the way. They must walk where they can, and crawl where they cannot walk. (*Puts animal skin on his back and ties it around his neck*) And I am all their animals. Not very many, I am afraid, for Chih Yuan is not a very rich farmer. He has just enough to keep his family alive: a cow and two goats, maybe. Or perhaps two cows and one goat. Whichever it is, I am the animals. (*He ties a rope around his neck.*) With this rope, Chih Yuan will lead me over the mountain to safety. But now they are ready to go. (*He walks downstage right and stands there.* HAN HSIN, CHIH YUAN, KUAN-YIN, MIAO CHEN, *and* YAO *come out door marked "Entrance." They stand before the stepladder. Each has a very large pack tied to his back and walks stooped.*)

CHIH YUAN: We are ready then.

MIAO CHEN: I have said goodbye to my doll and bade her sleep until I return.

YAO: And I have said goodbye to my kite and Chou.

CHIH YUAN (*To* HAN HSIN): Will you go first, Wise Old Man, and lead the way?

HAN HSIN: It is best that I do. (*He climbs over the stepladder.*)

CHIH YUAN: And honored Wife, you follow him, taking my children with you.

KUANYIN: I shall follow the wise Han Hsin. (*She climbs over the stepladder, followed by* MIAO CHEN *and* YAO.)

CHIH YUAN: I shall bring the animals. (CHIH YUAN *takes the rope and leads the* PROPERTY MAN, *as they both climb over the ladder. When the* PROPERTY MAN *reaches the top of the ladder, he sits on the top step.*)

PROPERTY MAN: So all day and all night, for many days, the wise old man, Han Hsin, and the family of Chih Yuan climbed the mountain. Sometimes they stopped for rest.

HAN HSIN (*From back of the ladder*): We shall rest here for the night. It is too dark to go on.

PROPERTY MAN: Sometimes they found food in the mountains: snails, eggs of the mountain birds, lizards.

CHIH YUAN: Eat quickly, my children, for soon we must start climbing again.

PROPERTY MAN: Sometimes they found little beauties where they were least expected.

KUANYIN: Look, my Husband, a little flower here among the rocks.

CHIH YUAN: Perhaps our little daughter would like to wear it in her hair until we stop tonight.

MIAO CHEN: I wish that I could bring it back to my doll.

YAO: I wish that Chou were here to see it.

PROPERTY MAN: But most of the time, they climb. And the sun beats down by day, and the cold mountain winds blow at night. And their feet and their arms ache. But finally they reach the top, and there they stay until spring comes, and the frost is gone. Then they climb back down the mountain and return home. (*The* PROPERTY MAN *climbs over the back of the ladder, and then turns the ladder around so that the back now faces the audience. And all of the actors climb over the ladder again, coming downstage, in the same order in which they had climbed up the mountain.*)

HAN HSIN: We have returned to the good earth, and the earth has returned to life. You see, it is spring here in the valley, and the frost is gone.

CHIH YUAN: But underneath the life is the dead grass, and that is where we would be too, Wise Old Man, if you had not come to us. The family of Chih Yuan is most grateful.

HAN HSIN: This old man is grateful to the family of Chih Yuan for all the services they have rendered to him through this long winter.

KUANYIN: If my honored husband will permit, this lowly wife will now set her house in order.

CHIH YUAN: It is good to be home, is it not, Wife?

KUANYIN: It is good, my Husband. (*She starts for door marked "Exit."*)

MIAO CHEN: And I will go with you, my Mother, to see if my doll stayed warm and asleep all winter and safe from the killing frost. (KUANYIN *and* MIAO CHEN *go through "Exit" door.*)

PROPERTY MAN (*Taking off animal robe and picking up stepladder*): Now the animals are back in their pens, and I am once again your Property Man. And so I shall move the mountain from your sight so that you may forget the hard winter behind and think only of the warm spring and pleasant summer ahead. (*He bows to the audience and moves off-stage right.*)

YAO: Honored Father, may I visit my kite?

CHIH YUAN: Is home merely a place where my young son flies his kite?

YAO: No, Honored Father, but I have a special reason.

CHIH YUAN: You may go, my Son. (YAO *bows and exits through "Exit" door.*) He has not mentioned his turtle in many days now, Wise Old Man. Do you think that he has forgotten?

HAN HSIN: It is to be hoped for. The short memory of youth is healing ointment for the pains of growing up.

CHIH YUAN: It was hard of me not to let him take his turtle.

HAN HSIN: It was hard, but only a hard man can live in times of danger. Is it not so?

CHIH YUAN: I shall find comfort in your words.

HAN HSIN: Find more than that in the experience. When the killing frost comes again on the ninth day of the ninth month, be prepared. Do not let the summer sun tell you that life will always be kind.

CHIH YUAN: Even in the midst of plenty, I shall try to remember. It is hard to dwell on one's evil days, but I shall try to remember.

HAN HSIN: Do not mark them down as evil days. Evil days are only those that leave us less than we were, not those that leave us with less than we had. Mark down in your memory the day of our departure—the Double Nine—the ninth day of the ninth month. And celebrate it.

CHIH YUAN: Celebrate it? I am indeed a simple man, Wise Old Man, but why should I celebrate the coming of the killing frost, the flight from my home, the day that I had to turn a hard face against my son's request?

HAN HSIN: If you mark it as a day of celebration, you will love to think upon it; and the Double Nine will then be the day upon which your labors for the year are completed, the day you are prepared for the winter. Make it a day of laughter, dancing, singing, and special feasting. Make it a celebration of the day that you conquered evil.

CHIH YUAN: Han Hsin is indeed a wise man. I shall forever keep the celebration of the Double Nine, and I shall be grateful. But I shall be sad, too, for in my celebration I shall remember that on this day, my son had to learn that in the midst of the struggle of life, a friend had to be sacrificed. And such a small friend, too. Poor Chou. (MIAO CHEN *comes out "Entrance" door, carrying her doll.*)

MIAO CHEN (*Holding doll up*): See, Father, my doll. She is just as good as when we left.

HAN HSIN: Even better, Small Daughter, for she has had a long winter's nap.

MIAO CHEN: That is true, Wise Old Man, and she will be able to play all the harder this summer for it.

CHIH YUAN: Are you happy, my Daughter?

MIAO CHEN: Very happy, my Father. (*She bows and exits through "Exit" door.*)

HAN HSIN: The young find happiness so easily.

CHIH YUAN: And sometimes lose it so quickly.

HAN HSIN: You are still unhappy about your small son's turtle.

CHIH YUAN: Even now, he stands alone somewhere grieving for his lost friend. (YAO *comes running out of the "Entrance" door and runs into his father.*)

YAO: Oh, I . . . .

CHIH YUAN: Is this my son? Or has someone left the gate of the goat pen unlatched?

YAO: Miserable son is unhappy to have caused honored father trouble.

CHIH YUAN: Why are you running with your eyes shut?

YAO: It is my kite, Honored Father.

CHIH YUAN: Your kite? It still flies, and you are anxious to fly it? Well, you may.

YAO: Yes, Honored Father, and more than that. It has flown all winter.

CHIH YUAN: Flown all winter? Small son will be so good as to explain.

YAO: It has flown all winter above the killing frost, and it has kept my friend safe.

CHIH YUAN: Young son will please stop bouncing around like kite in whirlwind and explain.

YAO: Young son tied his turtle to the kite when we left, and he is still alive. (*Reaches inside blouse and pulls out turtle*) See, Father. Chou!

CHIH YUAN (*Looking at the turtle and touching it*) Chou? So it is. (*Speaking to turtle*) So, Chou, you have turned bird and escaped the killing frost. It is a remarkable thing. And to think of a kite flying all winter long.

HAN HSIN: I must leave now, Chih Yuan. But do not forget my advice to celebrate the Double Nine—with all the merriment you know.

CHIH YUAN: I shall remember, and the family of Chih Yuan will be greatly honored if you will bless us with your presence for the celebration.

HAN HSIN: I shall come if. . . .

CHIH YUAN: If?

HAN HSIN: If small son will make the Double Nine the occasion for demonstrating his remarkable powers with the kite.

CHIH YUAN: Kites shall fill the air. It shall be each year a part of our celebration. (*All three bow and leave through door marked "Exit."*)

PROPERTY MAN: Thus it came about that each year on the ninth day of the ninth month, the Chinese celebrated the coming of winter with the Feast of the Double Nine, and kites filled the air. And now, honored audience, our little play is finished, and we hope that it has met with your approval. If so, please indicate by pressing your hands together thus. (*He claps his hands.*) Worthless Property Man thanks you. (*Bows and exits off stage right. The gong rings.*)

THE END

ROBIN HOOD AND THE MATCH
AT NOTTINGHAM
(*England*)

> Come listen to me, you gallants so free,
> All you that love mirth for to hear,
> And I will tell you of a bold outlaw,
> That lived in Nottinghamshire.

So begins an old English ballad, just one of thousands of stories told in song, in poetry and in prose about the famous outlaw of Sherwood Forest, Robin Hood. If one were to read all of these, one would soon find that there were two Robin Hoods. One lived about eight hundred years ago, and not much is actually known about him. Some think he was a nobleman; others think he was a poor widow's son. But all seem to agree that he was the leader of a band of outlaws who robbed the rich to help the poor.

The second Robin Hood is the one most of us know best. He was the best archer in England, the best friend the poor ever had, and an unrelenting foe of the Sheriff of Nottingham, Prince John's henchman. This Robin Hood was a witty fellow who loved justice above all and a good joke next best. He gathered around him a group of colorful followers—Little John, who was far from little; Friar Tuck, who looked like a barrel and was strong as an oak; Allan-a-Dale, who made up songs about Robin Hood and his Merry Men; Will Scarlet; Maid Marian.

It is about this second Robin Hood that this play is written. It is not from recorded history but from an old English ballad that the episode of the shooting match at Nottingham Town is taken. No one knows whether or not it is true, but it is the kind of story that symbolizes the spirit of Robin Hood and "Merrie England."

Robin Hood and the Match
at Nottingham

Characters

ROBIN HOOD (Jock o' Teviotdale)
ADAM O' THE DELL   } *the three archers*
GILBERT O' THE RED CAP

THE SHERIFF OF NOTTINGHAM
PRINCE JOHN
FRIAR TUCK
LITTLE JOHN
ALLAN-A-DALE (Lincoln Green)
MAID MARIAN
QUEEN ELINOR
LADIES-IN-WAITING
COURTIERS
TOWNSPEOPLE

SETTING: *The fair at Nottingham.*

AT RISE: *The* LADIES-IN-WAITING, COURTIERS *and* TOWNS-
PEOPLE *sit on two rows of benches at right.* ALLAN-A-
DALE, *who is disguised as "Lincoln Green," stands
strumming his lyre and singing. The others listen and
then join in the chorus.*

ALLAN-A-DALE (*Singing*)*:

> Come listen to me, you gallants so free,
> All you that love mirth to hear,
> And I will tell of a bold outlaw,
> That lived in Nottinghamshire.

ALL (*Chorus*): That lived in Nottinghamshire.

ALLAN-A-DALE (*Singing*):

> As Robin Hood in the forest stood,
> All under the greenwood tree,
> There he saw a brave young man,
> As fine as fine might be.

ALL (*Chorus*): Robin Hood. Robin Hood. As fine as fine might be. (PRINCE JOHN *and the* SHERIFF OF NOTTINGHAM *rush out of the tent.*)

PRINCE JOHN: Who is doing this singing?

SHERIFF: It isn't singing, Prince John. It's treason. He was singing about Robin Hood.

PRINCE JOHN: I heard him. I heard them all. "Robin Hood. Robin Hood. As fine as fine might be." I'll have some heads for this.

SHERIFF (*Grabbing* ALLAN-A-DALE): And this must be the villain, Prince John, for he has the lyre in his hand.

PRINCE JOHN: A lyre in his hand and a lie in his throat. Take him to the tower, and we'll be rid of both.

ROBIN HOOD (*Calling from the crowd*): One moment, Your Majesty, please.

PRINCE JOHN (*Looking about*): Who shouted that? (*A*

---

* The tune of an old English ballad may be used here, or a traditional Robin Hood song may be substituted.

tattered stranger, ROBIN HOOD, *comes forward. He is poorly dressed, and one eye is covered with a black patch.*)

ROBIN HOOD: Meaning no offense, Your Majesty, I did.

PRINCE JOHN: And who are you? Or should I say, *what* are you? By your appearance, I would guess that you are something the village cats think not worth eating.

ROBIN HOOD: Men call me Jock o' Teviotdale, and I do come here to shoot for the prize the Sheriff has offered for the best archer. I hope to win the Golden Arrow.

SHERIFF: A one-eyed archer? Good heavens!

ROBIN HOOD: I don't pull the bow with my eyes, Sheriff, but with my hands and arms.

ADAM O' THE DELL: And a right honest archer he is, too, Sheriff. There are only three of us left in the match— Gilbert o' the Red Cap, this fellow, and myself.

PRINCE JOHN: I don't care about all that. Why have you shouted for me to stop as I ordered this traitor to the tower? Are you one of Robin Hood's followers?

ROBIN HOOD: Not I, Sheriff. I have never seen the face of the man in my whole life.

PRINCE JOHN: You may count yourself lucky. It's an ugly face.

ROBIN HOOD: So I've been told, Your Majesty. As ugly as my own, and I never want to meet the man coming down the road who wears it. But I mean to speak for this poor minstrel here, poor Lincoln.

SHERIFF: Lincoln! I hate the name ever since Robin Hood and his followers started wearing Lincoln green.

ROBIN HOOD: Aye, Lincoln Green. That's the poor minstrel's name, and he hates the name like sin. In fact, he told me he was thinking of changing it very soon.

PRINCE JOHN: He'll have no need of changing it. We don't put names on the graves of traitors.

ROBIN HOOD: But poor old Lincoln's no traitor.

SHERIFF: We heard him sing the praises of Robin Hood.

ROBIN HOOD: He was singing about that villain, Robin Hood. But he wasn't singing his praises. He was singing about the time, soon to come, we all hope, when that knave and the brave Sheriff—it's yourself, I mean— stand face-to-face. Let him sing the chorus again and you shall see.

PRINCE JOHN: Let him sing and get on with it. All this bores me.

ALLAN-A-DALE: This is what I sang last. (*Sings*)

> As Robin Hood in the forest stood,
> All under the greenwood tree,
> There he saw a brave young man,
> As fine as fine might be.

ROBIN HOOD: Your honors will note that it is "the brave young man" who is as fine as fine might be. Not Robin Hood. And who do you think that brave young man is? Why it's you, yourself, Sheriff. You probably did not recognize yourself.

PRINCE JOHN: As a "brave, young man," I would not recognize him either. All right, you are pardoned this time, singer. But save your voice to sing the praises of your king hereafter.

ALLAN-A-DALE: That I will, my Lord. That I will.

PRINCE JOHN: Now, get this shooting match over with. My money is on Gilbert o' the Red Cap. Sheriff, you bet on Adam o' the Dell.

SHERIFF: But I think Gilbert will win.

PRINCE JOHN: Of course, he will win. That's why I'm betting on him.

ROBIN HOOD: And will no one bet on me?

PRINCE JOHN: No one. Not even your own mother, I should think. (LITTLE JOHN *steps forward.*)

LITTLE JOHN: I'll bet with Jock, Your Majesty.

PRINCE JOHN: Good heavens, man, what for? The fellow has only one eye and no brains.

LITTLE JOHN: We beggars should stick together.

PRINCE JOHN: If you bet on him, you'll always be a beggar. But I'll take your wager. Gilbert over one-eyed Jock. It's a bet. Where's your money?

LITTLE JOHN: I have only a single coin, Your Majesty. (*Holding coin up*)

PRINCE JOHN: I'll take it. (*Grabbing it*) Every penny counts when you're a king.

FRIAR TUCK (*Coming forward*): Shall I hold the wagers, Prince John?

PRINCE JOHN: Friar Tuck! What are you doing here? I would expect you to be with your thieving friend, Robin Hood.

FRIAR TUCK: The church is a friend of all, even thieves. As you shall find, Prince John, when you need our comfort. Shall I hold your wager?

PRINCE JOHN (*Giving it to him*): All right, take it.

FRIAR TUCK: And your coin, too, Prince John?

PRINCE JOHN: Sheriff, give him a coin.

SHERIFF (*Giving* FRIAR TUCK *a coin*): No matter which of you wins, I shall lose.

PRINCE JOHN: Let's get on with the match. I haven't all day to watch beggars at play. If you all have such time to waste, you must have more than you have been paying taxes on. (ROBIN HOOD, GILBERT, AND ADAM *go up to the platform.* LITTLE JOHN *and* FRIAR TUCK *stand downstage right.* PRINCE JOHN, *the* SHERIFF, MAID MARIAN, *and* QUEEN ELINOR *stand downstage left by the tent. The rest of the people sit on the benches.*)

SHERIFF: All right, let the last match begin.

GILBERT (*Calling from the platform*): We have no judge here, Sheriff.

SHERIFF: Very well, I will judge.

PRINCE JOHN: No, you won't! You are betting on Adam. I will judge.

QUEEN ELINOR: And you, my son, are betting on Gilbert. A third party would be better.

PRINCE JOHN: I am a Prince, and I say I will judge.

QUEEN ELINOR: And I am a Queen and your mother, and I say you shouldn't. Here, we shall let Maid Marian judge. She has bet neither on Gilbert nor Adam.

PRINCE JOHN: She has bet on Robin Hood who isn't even entered. But, it suits me. Let Maid Marian judge, for no matter who wins, I will win from her. (*To* MARIAN) The next time, young lady, you will not place your trust in an outlaw.

MARIAN: The match is not yet over, Prince John. Robin Hood may yet arrive to shoot in the match and win the Golden Arrow. (*She walks up to the platform.*)

SHERIFF (*To* PRINCE JOHN): I hope she's right. I hope Robin Hood does appear. I have my men spread throughout the woods, and they'll give him more arrows in his hide than a porcupine has quills, if he but show his face.

PRINCE JOHN: My dear, silly Sheriff, I have told you many times. Robin Hood won't appear. The man's a coward.

Why I'd match old one-eyed Jock against your terror of Sherwood Forest for courage. If Robin Hood had intended to come, he'd have been here by now.

SHERIFF: Maybe yes and maybe no. Friar Tuck is here, and that makes me suspicious.

PRINCE JOHN: Friar Tuck likes thieves, and he's come to visit you, Sheriff. It's perfectly natural.

SHERIFF: Prince John, I am your loyal follower.

PRINCE JOHN: I believe it. That's why I know you must be a thief. Let us fool all of England, Sheriff. But there is no need to fool ourselves.

SHERIFF: That hurts me. (*Taps his chest*) Here.

QUEEN ELINOR: Quiet, you two, with your whispering. Maid Marian is about to speak.

SHERIFF: Yes, Your Royal Majesty.

PRINCE JOHN: Yes, Mother. (MAID MARIAN *stands on the platform, facing the audience. The three archers stand back of her with their bows ready.*)

MARIAN: Ladies and Gentlemen, we now come to the last match of the day. And soon we shall see who shall win the Golden Arrow. There are but three left: Adam o' the Dell. . . .

SHERIFF: Shoot straight and true, Adam. (*Some of the crowd ad-lib encouragement, calling "Hooray for Adam!" "We're for you, Adam," etc.*)

MARIAN: Gilbert o' the Red Cap. . . .

PRINCE JOHN: We're for you, Gilbert. (*Some of the crowd ad-lib encouragement, calling ".Hooray for Gilbert," etc.*)

MARIAN: And the last of the three, Jock o' Teviotdale. (*There is complete silence; and then a few laugh.*) What, will no one cheer for Jock? Then I'll give him a cheer myself. Hooray for Jock! Shoot straight and true.

LITTLE JOHN: I'll join you in that, my Lady. Shoot straight, Jock. I've got a bet on you. (JOCK *gives a deep bow.*)

MARIAN: Each of these brave archers will shoot three arrows at the target one hundred yards distant there, and he whose arrows come the closest to the ring, shall win the prize. First comes Adam o' the Dell.

SHERIFF (*Shouts*): Shoot well, Adam, and if yours be the best shaft, a dozen silver pennies will I give you besides the prize.

ADAM: Truly, I will do my best. A man can do nothing more than that, but I will try. (ADAM *draws his bow and pretends to shoot. The crowd rises to its feet, and looks offstage to the left, following the "arrow."*)

SHERIFF: A good shot, Adam. It is barely two hands from the center. You will be a rich man yet. (*Some of the crowd ad-lib "A fair hit!" etc.*)

MARIAN: Adam o' the Dell placed his arrow two hands from the center. Now shoots Gilbert o' the Red Cap.

PRINCE JOHN: Best that mark and win a Prince's favor, Gilbert.

FIRST COURTIER: Ho for Gilbert o' the Red Cap!

GILBERT: As Adam said, a man can only do his best. And I shall try. (*He takes his place and pretends to shoot. The crowd again looks offstage to the left, following the "arrow."*)

SECOND COURTIER: He beat Adam's mark.

FIRST LADY: He is but a single hand away.

PRINCE JOHN: There, Sheriff, have you ever seen such shooting as that?

SHERIFF: Indeed I know only one man that can do so well. Robin Hood. Is it possible, Prince John, that Gilbert o' the Red Cap is none other than Robin Hood in disguise?

QUEEN ELINOR: Robin is almost a head taller.

PRINCE JOHN: And his shoulders are two inches broader. No, Sheriff, Gilbert is an honest archer and my champion. Don't try to get out of our bet.

MARIAN: Gilbert o' the Red Cap placed his arrow one hand from the center. Now shoots Jock o' Teviotdale.

THIRD COURTIER: We'd all better duck. He's bound to miss the target and hit one of us

FOURTH COURTIER: Lead him to the target, Maid Marian, for he cannot see it. Ho, Ho, Ho.

LITTLE JOHN: Quiet and give the poor fellow a chance.

PRINCE JOHN: I'm afraid that you've lost your wager, my friend. But let him shoot. (ROBIN HOOD *steps up and then pretends to shoot. The crowd leaps to its feet.*)

SHERIFF: The one-eyed man beat them both! His shot is but three fingers from the center.

LITTLE JOHN: No, it's only two.

QUEEN ELINOR: It looks as though you, Prince John, and you, Sheriff, have picked the wrong man. The one-eyed man shoots well.

PRINCE JOHN: It was but a lucky hit. He won't do it again.

SHERIFF: The fellow is lucky even to see the target, let alone hit it. There are two more shots. He won't win.

MAID MARIAN: The winner of the first round: Jock o' Teviotdale. His arrow is but two fingers from the center. And now for the second round, Adam o' the Dell. (ADAM *pretends to shoot again. The crowd rises.*)

SHERIFF: He beat Gilbert.

LITTLE JOHN: Aye, but not Jock.

MARIAN: Second shot for Adam o' the Dell—four fingers. Next. Gilbert o' the Red Cap. (GILBERT *shoots. The crowd rises.*)

PRINCE JOHN: A bad shot. It is almost two hands away.

MARIAN: Gilbert o' the Red Cap. One hand, four inches. Now shoots Jock o' Teviotdale. And if he places his arrow closer than Adam's, he wins with two victories out of three. (ROBIN HOOD *shoots. The crowd gasps.*)

SHERIFF: He missed the target.

LITTLE JOHN: He missed it completely.

SHERIFF (*Shouting*): You should have closed the other eye, Old One-Eye.

PRINCE JOHN: Ho, ho, Sheriff! Perhaps the one-eyed archer is Robin Hood. (*He laughs heartily.*) Robin Hood in a disguise—of course!

SHERIFF: Robin Hood's dog can shoot better than that.

MARIAN: A miss for Jock o' Teviotdale. Now, the last round. Scores so far: one first for Jock o' Teviotdale and one for Adam o' the Dell. If Adam takes a first, the prize is his. If Gilbert scores a first, it is a tie. And. . . .

PRINCE JOHN: And if old Jock even hits the target, it's a miracle. (*Crowd laughs.*)

MARIAN: And if Jock o' Teviotdale scores the first, he wins the Golden Arrow. Adam is the first to shoot.

SHERIFF: Shoot steady, Adam. (ADAM *rises and shoots. The crowd rises.*) It's a good shot. Only a hand away. Adam could win the Golden Arrow.

MARIAN: Adam's arrow is one hand away. Now Gilbert o' the Red Cap shoots (GILBERT *shoots, and crowd roars.*)

PRINCE JOHN: A direct hit! Gilbert wins the arrow. (*To* GILBERT) Good shooting, Gilbert. You have won many a wager for me today. (*To* FRIAR TUCK) I'll have my winnings, Friar Tuck.

FRIAR TUCK: You have not yet won, Prince John.

PRINCE JOHN: He hit the center, a direct hit. It counts double and gives him two points to the others' ones. Certainly I have won.

FRIAR TUCK: Not yet, Prince John. Jock still has one arrow left to shoot.

PRINCE JOHN: Good heavens, he can't win unless he can split Gilbert's arrow down the center.

SHERIFF: Which would be a neat trick for a man with a dozen eyes and impossible for a man with one.

FRIAR TUCK: And yet he's to have his chance, is he not?

PRINCE JOHN: All right, get it over with.

QUEEN ELINOR: Patience, son. The people hate to think their ruler is a poor sport.

PRINCE JOHN: The people hate me anyway, and I hate them. We did not give this match for their amusement, but only to trap Robin Hood.

SHERIFF: Who was too much of a coward to come.

MARIAN: And now for the last shot of the contest: Jock o' Teviotdale. (ROBIN HOOD *raises his bow quickly and shoots. Crowd shouts.*)

QUEEN ELINOR: Good heavens, he did it. He split Gilbert's arrow.

SHERIFF: The one-eyed beggar has won!

PRINCE JOHN: It isn't fair. There must be a run-off. It was just luck.

GILBERT: My lord, I never shot better in my life. Twenty years have I shot shaft, and never have I shot a finer arrow. But this fellow, Jock o' Teviotdale, could give me lessons for a thousand years, and I could never match his skill. No, my Lord, it is not luck. He is the winner, and I will shoot no more today.

PRINCE JOHN: You'll do as you're told!

QUEEN ELINOR: Be careful, my son. If you arouse the sense of fair play in your countrymen, you may have a revolution on your hands.

PRINCE JOHN: You may be right, Mother. (*Aloud.*) I quite agree with Gilbert o' the Red Cap. We have seen a great victory here today, and anyway I win from the Sheriff. Gilbert beat his man, and I win from Maid Marian, too.

SHERIFF (*Taking a golden arrow and carrying it to* ROBIN HOOD): And we have today found a man who can out-shoot Robin Hood. (*Gives arrow to* ROBIN HOOD) What's more, Jock, today I offer you a place in my service. I will clothe you better than you have ever dressed, and you shall eat and drink the best. Every Christmas, you shall get fourscore silver pennies for your pay. I do declare that you are a better archer than that same coward, Robin Hood, who did not dare to show his face here today. Well, good fellow, will you join my service?

ROBIN HOOD: No, that I will not. I will be my own master, and no man in merry England shall send me on an errand.

SHERIFF: Then get out of here, and may the devil take you. I have a good mind to have you beaten for your insolence. (*He turns and walks back to* PRINCE JOHN. ROBIN HOOD, FRIAR TUCK, LITTLE JOHN *and* ALLAN-A-DALE *exit upstage right.*)

PRINCE JOHN: And you, Marian. Don't forget to pay your wager. Robin Hood was not here today.

MARIAN (*Laughing*): Do you know, Prince John, that the big fellow to whom you lost your bet was Little John?

PRINCE JOHN: What! That villain Robin Hood's right-hand man. Where is he? Where is he?

QUEEN ELINOR: You might as well be calm, son. He's disappeared; he left with Friar Tuck.

PRINCE JOHN: Aye, that Tuck! If he weren't a friar, I'd have him frying in his own fat.

SHERIFF (*Jumping up and down in anger*): Now I know who that singer was. He was no Lincoln Green, but he wears it! It was Allan-a-Dale, Robin Hood's minstrel.

MARIAN: Jock said he didn't like his name and could change it quickly.

SHERIFF: I'd like to get my hands on his throat.

QUEEN ELINOR: You won't today, Sheriff. I saw him leave with the others.

PRINCE JOHN: I suppose we should be grateful, Sheriff, Robin Hood didn't come, or with your usual stupidity, you'd have lent him your purse. Fools! I'm surrounded by nothing but fools.

SHERIFF: Robin Hood's a coward, Prince John. I've made mistakes, but Robin Hood will never fool me. I'd have caught him today if he hadn't been a coward. (*A horn blows off. Everyone jumps up.*)

FIRST COURTIER: What's that?

SECOND COURTIER: It's Robin Hood's horn. He's here somewhere.

THIRD COURTIER: What fell in that bush? (*He reaches behind a bush, and holds up a golden arrow.*)

PRINCE JOHN (*Turning upstage*): Look. An arrow!

SHERIFF: The Golden Arrow. The prize I gave to Jock o' Teviotdale.

FIRST LADY: Who shot it?

SECOND LADY: Look! It carries a message.

SHERIFF (*Taking arrow and message*): I'll read it.

PRINCE JOHN (*Taking it*): I'll read it. (*Reading*) "To the Sheriff of Nottingham: Good Sheriff, sweet Sheriff, do you consider it honest to pass out bronzed wood for a golden arrow?" (*To* SHERIFF) You rogue, you cheated on the prize. (*Continues reading*) "I was sure you meant well, so I took your purse from your belt to pay for an arrow of gold. I was sure you'd want me to have it."

SHERIFF (*Holding belt*): My purse! My purse! It is gone!

PRINCE JOHN: But there's worse to come. Listen: "But there's one thing you should know. Your plan to trap Robin Hood, your old foe, worked well, for he was the one who won the prize today."

SHERIFF: That one-eyed beggar was Robin Hood in disguise! He tricked me, he tricked me!

MARIAN: And you, Prince John, lost the wager to me. It was Robin Hood who won today.

CROWD (*Laughs and starts to sing*): "Come listen to me, you gallants so free! And I will tell you of a bold outlaw. . . ."

PRINCE JOHN: Quiet, all of you.

CROWD (*Singing louder*): "Robin Hood. Robin Hood, that beat the Sheriff in Nottingham Town."

PRINCE JOHN (*Grabbing Sheriff's ear and leading him off toward tent*): It's all your fault, you fool.

SHERIFF: But, Your Majesty! How was I to know? He tricked me. (PRINCE JOHN *and* SHERIFF *exit into tent*.)

CROWD (*Singing*): "Robin Hood. Robin Hood, that beat the Sheriff in Nottingham Town." (*Curtain*)

THE END

THE FRENCH CABINETMAKER
(France)

This farce is set in France. The general plot for the play is taken from an old seventeenth-century French farce, *Crispin Medecin*, by Noel de Breton. Although the farce is, in part, a development from the Italian *commedia del' arte*, as a modern dramatic form it is uniquely French. The word *farce*, in fact, is from a French word meaning "stuffing." And that is exactly how the French thought of the farce: a play "stuffed" with tricks and pranks, disguises, physical violence without physical pain, exaggerated characters.

So much of French literature is in the "grand manner," formal dramatic poetry in which exalted characters speak only the refined language of sentiment, that France's role in the development and origin of farce may seem surprising. But during the 17th century, the theater of France was the theater of the court, and the theater of England was closed by the order of the government. Thus in both of these countries there was no professional stage for the common people. Wandering actors and clowns filled this gap, and thus the farce was born. It was the ideal play to take from place to place, and it was then—and is now—the kind of a play that people love to see. Farce doesn't teach a lesson, nor explain life logically. It has only one intention: to make people laugh.

In performing this play, the actors will find the best modern examples of the needed acting techniques in the dramas of the absurd and in such old movies as those with Laurel and Hardy. In the farce, the acting is external—showing how people *seem*, rather than how people are.

The French Cabinetmaker

Characters

ANGELICA
SUZETTE, *the giggling one*
MARIE, *the prim one*
AURELIA, *the sighing one*
MADAME JOSEPHINE, *Angelica's mother*
ADOLPHE JADIN, *Angelica's father*
CRISPIN, *Angelica's suitor*
ANDRE, *another suitor*

SETTING: *The workshop of Adolphe Jadin, the cabinet-maker. On the worktable are a broken chair, a folded checkered tablecloth, a large saw, and other tools.*
AT RISE: ANGELICA *is standing downstage, talking to her three friends,* SUZETTE, MARIE, *and* AURELIA, *each of whom reacts according to her nature—giggling, sternly disapproving, and sighing.*

ANGELICA: And Papa says that two suitors are like spring and fall. No matter which one you have, you'll wish that you had the other.

SUZETTE (*Giggling*): Your Papa is so funny. He can't see anything without his glasses; yet he always pretends he can. Do you remember the day he thought that the horse of Broussard the Baker was Madame Broussard?

AURELIA: And he told her that he had never seen her look better. No wonder Madame Broussard broke the plate over your Papa's head. Broussard the Baker has the ugliest horse in town.

MARIE (*Sternly*): This is no laughing matter, you two foolish things. Angelica has a problem having two suitors.

AURELIA (*Sighing*): I wish I had such a problem. I have only one suitor, and he doesn't suit me at all. Oh, I'd love to be in love.

MARIE: This is no time for foolish talk about love. Having two suitors can cause all sorts of trouble. Why a thing like that can go to a silly girl's head.

ANGELICA: I have only one suitor—Crispin. It is only Papa who insists that I must accept Andre as a suitor, too.

MARIE: You are making a mistake, Angelica. Forget Crispin. Andre is the one for you.

AURELIA: But Crispin is handsome and Andre is ugly.

SUZETTE: Crispin says funny things, but Andre just says stupid ones.

ANGELICA: Crispin is kinder, and even Papa says he is the better worker.

MARIE: Exactly! No matter how you look at it, Crispin *looks* better. There must be something wrong with anyone who looks perfect. Take Andre and let Crispin go.

ANGELICA: I could never do that. I love Crispin, and besides it would break his heart.

MARIE: Nonsense! No one really ever dies of a broken heart.

AURELIA: I would.

MARIE: Two days after you married Andre, Crispin would have another girl.

SUZETTE (*Giggling*): I would be glad to marry him. He would make me laugh all the time.

MARIE: He doesn't need a silly goose, and you don't need anyone to make you laugh.

AURELIA: I would be glad to marry him. (*Sighs*) He is so handsome.

MARIE: He doesn't need a foolish sighing girl, and you don't need anyone to be in love with. You're in love with love.

SUZETTE: If I am too silly. . . .

AURELIA: And I too foolish. . . .

TOGETHER: Who will marry Crispin?

MARIE: It just so happens I am very fond of Angelica.

SUZETTE: Yes?

MARIE: And Angelica is very fond of Crispin.

AURELIA: Yes?

MARIE (*Looking as if she is making a sacrifice*): So I suppose the only thing to do is to marry Crispin myself. (*The other girls laugh.*)

ANGELICA: I will marry Crispin, Marie. Mama says so. But you may have Andre with my best wishes.

MARIE: Ha! I would never marry anyone as stupid, mean, and ugly as Andre.

SUZETTE: Why doesn't your Papa like Crispin, Angelica?

ANGELICA: Papa loves Crispin. But he says that a father has to make sure that when his daughter picks a husband she doesn't make a mistake. And Papa says the only way to be sure I don't make a bad choice is not to let me make a choice at all. So I cannot marry either Crispin or Andre until one of them stops being a suitor.

AURELIA: Haven't you told Andre you don't want to marry him?

ANGELICA: Yes. (*Sighs*) Many times. But he says that when a man is as ugly, stupid, and mean as he is, he can't be bothered as to whether the girl wants to marry him. He said he wouldn't marry a girl who was so stupid as to want to marry him.

MARIE: He's right. Andre is very smart in a stupid sort of way. And he will win you yet because Crispin will one day get tired of waiting.

ANGELICA: To make it worse, Papa has now said that I am not to see either of them until one of them goes away. (*Enter* MADAME JOSEPHINE.)

JOSEPHINE: Pinch your cheeks, Angelica, to make them glow. I saw a sly fox in the yard eyeing my little chick.

ANGELICA (*Pinching her cheeks to rouge them*): Mama, is Crispin coming to see me?

JOSEPHINE: You were expecting maybe the King of France or the Duke of Normandy? You know Crispin is coming. I can see your eyes sparkle.

AURELIA: Then I guess we'd better go.

SUZETTE: I guess so, but I should like to stay and listen. He says such funny things.

MARIE: I think we should stay. You shouldn't see Crispin if your Papa says not to.

JOSEPHINE: Go home and tell your mother she wants you, Marie.

MARIE: Well! I guess I know what you mean. I'm leaving. (*Exit* MARIE.)

AURELIA: Good luck, Angelica.

SUZETTE: If he says anything funny, Angelica, remember it and tell me tomorrow. (AURELIA *and* SUZETTE *exit*.)

JOSEPHINE: The cackling geese have gone, and now this old hen had better fly, too. Do not let him stay too long. Your Papa will be back soon, and if he sees Crispin here, he will become angry and make you marry Andre.

ANGELICA: Oh, Mama, that must never happen.

JOSEPHINE: Then you be careful. I shall be outside looking for your Papa, and I will warn you when I see him returning. (*Exit* JOSEPHINE.)

ANGELICA (*Following her to the door*): Thank you, Mama. When Papa comes, yell loud because I will not be listening. (CRISPIN *comes in the other door*.)

CRISPIN: Angelica!

ANGELICA: Crispin! (*In this routine, they advance toward each other, one stiff step at a time, each calling the other's name as they draw nearer together. The actors are to take each step only as they speak. When they finally reach each other, it should be in the middle of a step; and they should stand fixed like statues for a few seconds and then go slowly into the action.*)

CRISPIN: Angelica!

ANGELICA: Crispin!

CRISPIN: Angelica!

ANGELICA: Crispin!

CRISPIN: Angelica!

BOTH (*Coming together*): Angelica! Crispin!

CRISPIN: How have you been, Angelica?

ANGELICA: Pretty good, Crispin. How have *you* been?

CRISPIN: Pretty good. How's your mother?

ANGELICA: Pretty good. How's *your* mother?

CRISPIN: Pretty good. How's your father?

ANGELICA: Pretty good. How's *your* father?

CRISPIN: Pretty good. How are your aunts and uncles?

ANGELICA: Pretty good. How are *your* aunts and uncles?

CRISPIN: Pretty good. (*Pause*) Uncle Louie has the gout.

ANGELICA: Oh?

CRISPIN: Aunt Ellie has lumbago.

ANGELICA: Oh?

CRISPIN: Uncle Pierre has the seven-year itch.

ANGELICA: Oh?

CRISPIN: But they're all pretty good. (*Sighs*)

ANGELICA (*Sighing as she puts her hands in his*): Alone!

CRISPIN: Alone at last!

ANGELICA: At last alone! (ANDRE *sticks his head through the upstage window.*)

ANDRE: Oh, no, you're not. There are three of us. (*He points his finger at each as he counts them off.*) One. Two. (*Counts them again*) One. Two. Well, I thought there were three of us. But at least there are two of us, so nobody's alone.

ANGELICA: Andre! Why don't you go away?

ANDRE: I like it here.

CRISPIN: Don't you know when you're not wanted?

ANDRE: I'm not wanted any place.

ANGELICA: Oh, go away, Andre. (JOSEPHINE *opens door, left, sticks her head in.*)

JOSEPHINE: Crispin! Crispin, fly away. Papa is coming. (*She exits.*)

ANGELICA: Papa! Quick, go. If he finds you here, he will become angry and make me marry Andre.

ANDRE: Hey, that's a good idea. And I'd better hide so he doesn't find me, too. (ANDRE *disappears. The scene that follows should be done with a great deal of confusion, using the "clown stuff" of farce. The basic action is this:* CRISPIN *tries to get out door right before* ADOLPHE *comes in door left. He rushes first to door right, but* ANDRE *has locked it. Then he rushes toward door left, but he collides with* JOSEPHINE *who has come to help him. Then he grabs the tablecloth from the worktable and "disguises" himself as table. All of the movements are exaggerated and noisy, but each movement must be as exact and clear as a step in a dance.*)

CRISPIN (*Parting from* ANGELICA): I go.

ANGELICA: Yes, you must go.

CRISPIN: I don't want to go.

ANGELICA: I don't want you to go.

CRISPIN: But I must go.

ANGELICA: Yes, go.

JOSEPHINE: Go, Crispin, go! Papa comes. (CRISPIN *rushes to the door right, but turns back to* ANGELICA *with a sigh.*)

CRISPIN: I go.

ANGELICA (*Waving goodbye*): Yes, I know.

JOSEPHINE (*From door left*): Hurry and go. Here comes Papa.

CRISPIN (*Grabs the doorknob to leave, but the doorknob comes off in his hand, and he falls*): The door! (*He jumps up.*) The door is locked!

ANDRE (*Outside*): Ah ha, Crispin. Let's see you get out of this one.

CRISPIN (*Beating on the door*): Let me out. Andre, let me out!

ANDRE: Papa Jadin will let you out. With the toe of his boot.

JOSEPHINE (*Runs in from door left to help* CRISPIN): Get out. Get out, Crispin. Papa is coming.

ANGELICA (*Rushing to door left to take* JOSEPHINE's *place*): Hurry, you still have time. Papa has stopped to speak to the butcher's dog. He thinks it is Mademoiselle Fifi.

CRISPIN (*Rushes toward door left*): Maybe I can get out that door before he comes in. He cannot see. So if I bark when I pass him, he will think I am the butcher's dog. (*He collides with* JOSEPHINE. *She is not moved at all, but* CRISPIN *bounces back like a rubber ball off a stone wall. He lands on the floor.* JOSEPHINE *picks him up and sets him on his feet with a jump.*)

CRISPIN: Excuse me, Mama. I did not mean to hurt you.

ANGELICA (*Yelling from the door*): The dog just bit Papa on the nose.

JOSEPHINE (*Pushing* CRISPIN *one way and then pulling him the other*): Run. Hide. Stand still. Think. Run.

CRISPIN: Where will I hide?

ANDRE (*Sticking his head through the window and yelling*): Find a mouse hole and hide in that, you rat. (*He disappears again.*)

CRISPIN (*Grabs the tablecloth and puts it over himself*): I know. I'll pretend to be a table.

JOSEPHINE (*Helping him*): Yes. Yes. That will do it. (CRISPIN *stands straight, and* JOSEPHINE *spreads the tablecloth over him. He now stands, a very tall and slender table, in the middle of the stage.*)

ANGELICA: Hurry, Mama. Here comes Papa.

JOSEPHINE: Everything is ready. Papa will never guess that this innocent-looking table is really Crispin in disguise. (*She putters around, straightening out the cloth.*) I wish I had a bowl of flowers to put on the table.

CRISPIN: Make it a very small bowl, Mama. I have a weak head.

JOSEPHINE: Quiet! Tables do not talk. (CRISPIN *stands very still, and the two pretend to be unconcerned. ADOLPHE JADIN enters with a great deal of excitement. He has one hand on his nose.*)

ADOLPHE: Do you know what Mlle. Fifi just did? She bit me right on the nose.

ANGELICA: Mlle. Fifi bit you on the nose, Papa?

ADOLPHE: Yes, she did. She is a very pretty woman, I must admit, but does that mean she should bite me on the nose, I ask you?

JOSEPHINE: Did you say anything you shouldn't have said, Papa?

ADOLPHE (*Performing each action as he talks*): I simply tipped my hat, like this, bowed from the waist and said, "How are you this bright day, Mlle. Fifi?" And she bit me on the nose.

ANGELICA: Perhaps she was not feeling well, Papa.

ADOLPHE: That is probably so. Well, I'd better get to work. (*He puts his hat on CRISPIN.*) There is much to be done today: tables to make, tables to break. Much to be done. You two women had better run along. I shall be here until the sun goes down. (JOSEPHINE *and* ANGELICA *signal to each other, pointing to* CRISPIN, *and then* JOSEPHINE *nods knowingly.*)

JOSEPHINE: Papa, I have been thinking about Mlle. Fifi's biting you on the nose.

ADOLPHE (*Picking up a hammer from the worktable*): What is there to think about? It's done. She is a very pretty woman, and I suppose if she wants to bite me on the nose, it's her business. But I think it very unusual.

JOSEPHINE: I'll bet she did not know it was your nose she was biting. She has very weak eyes and cannot see without glasses.

ADOLPHE: Then why does she not wear glasses?

JOSEPHINE: She is proud, Papa. She does not want people to know that she cannot see without glasses.

ADOLPHE (*Picking up his hat and hitting it with the hammer*): That is very silly. If a person cannot see without glasses, he should wear glasses.

JOSEPHINE (*Watching him hit his hat*): What are you doing, Papa?

ADOLPHE: I am just knocking the dents out of this old pot. What do you think I am doing?

JOSEPHINE (*Taking the hammer and hat out of his hands*): You know, Papa, what you should do? You should go and tell Mlle. Fifi that you are sorry she bit your nose.

ADOLPHE: Yes, that is a good idea. She probably thought my nose was an apple, and she will be very disappointed now. I shall put on my hat and go. (*He picks up the broken chair from the worktable and puts it on his head.*) Well, Mama, let's go.

JOSEPHINE (*Taking off the chair and putting his hat on his head*): Just let me straighten your hat first. There, now it is fine. Let's go. (ADOLPHE *and* JOSEPHINE *start out the door together*.) And Angelica, you'd better get the place straightened up right away. We will return in a few minutes. (*Exit* ADOLPHE *and* JOSEPHINE.)

ANGELICA (*Going to* CRISPIN): It is all right now, Crispin. They are gone.

CRISPIN (*Takes off cloth and puts it back on the work-table*): Whew, it was hot under there. And when your Papa started talking about making and breaking tables, I thought my heart would stop. I am very glad that your Papa does not like to wear his glasses.

ANGELICA: Now, you'd better go, Crispin, before Papa returns.

CRISPIN: I know. I'll go.

ANGELICA: I don't want you to go.

CRISPIN: I know, but I must.

ANGELICA: You must, I know. So go.

CRISPIN (*Going to door left*): I go. But I shall return. (*Exit* CRISPIN.)

ANGELICA (*Addressing audience*): It's a funny sort of thing when a girl's in love. She seems to do nothing but say hello and goodbye. Now I'm very sure, because I've been told, that Crispin's very witty. And I know he's handsome because I love him very dearly. But for the life of me I can't remember a single thing he's ever said, except "Hello" and "I go." No wonder when people marry, they fall out of love. It's the only way they ever get a chance to talk to each other.

ANDRE (*Sticking his head in the window*): You can talk to me, Angelica.

ANGELICA: I don't want to talk to you.

ANDRE (*Climbing into the room*): You think Crispin very clever because he fooled your Papa.

ANGELICA: Cleverer than you.

ANDRE: I could do the same thing. But better. I look much more like a table than Crispin. (CRISPIN *is outside door left. He disguises himself to look like* ADOLPHE: *beard, long coat, hat. The audience, of course, knows who he is.*)

CRISPIN (*Calling from outside the door*): Daughter, I have come back. Mlle. Fifi was not at home.

ANGELICA (*To* ANDRE): If you think you can fool Papa, you'd better start now because here he is.

ANDRE (*Grabbing the tablecloth and covering himself*): Two can play the same game. (*He gets down on his hands and knees.*) Your Papa will think I am a table too. A better table than Crispin. (CRISPIN *enters.*)

CRISPIN (*Stamps in and grabs a hammer from the worktable*): Well, daughter, here I am. Fit and strong. I will have a fine time banging on my tables today. (*He hits the worktable with his hammer.*)

ANGELICA (*Making faces at* CRISPIN): Oh, Papa, you certainly are strong. You have muscles like Hercules. What table are you going to fix first, Papa? (*She points to* ANDRE.)

CRISPIN: Oh, I don't know. (*Going to* ANDRE) Oh, I think maybe I'll work on this little, squat, ugly table here. (*He pulls the cloth off* ANDRE.) See what an ugly table it is. (ANDRE *stays rigid, shivering.*) There seems to be something loose here. (*He boots* ANDRE *with the side of his shoe.* ANDRE *sprawls on his face, and then goes right back into position.*) Very wobbly too. This table will need a lot of hammering to get it into shape.

ANGELICA: Will you have to sand it, Papa?

CRISPIN: Down to the bone.

ANGELICA: Will you do any sawing, Papa?

CRISPIN: That's the first thing I must do, daughter. (*He takes the saw from the worktable.*) First, I must saw off this ugly knot. (*He pats* ANDRE's *head.*) It ruins the appearance of the whole table.

ANDRE (*Jumps up in terror*): It may be ugly. But it's my own. Angelica, I wanted to lose my head over you, but not this way. I'm leaving. (*Exit* ANDRE, *running.*)

CRISPIN (*Taking off the disguise*): I think we have seen the last of Andre now. If he keeps on moving at the same speed, he'll be in Spain before the sun goes down.

ANGELICA: Crispin, would you really have cut off his head?

CRISPIN: Just his ears. (ADOLPHE *and* JOSEPHINE *return. They can be heard outside door left.*)

ADOLPHE (*Outside*): Mlle. Fifi is a very pretty woman, Mama. But she should wear glasses.

ANGELICA (*Stage whisper*): It's Papa. What shall we do?

CRISPIN: We don't have to do anything now that I am your only suitor. (*Enter* ADOLPHE *and* JOSEPHINE. ADOLPHE *wears enormous glasses.*)

ANGELICA: Papa! You're wearing your glasses.

ADOLPHE: I do not really need them, but my wearing them might set an example for Mlle. Fifi.

JOSEPHINE: Mlle. Fifi did not even recognize Papa.

ADOLPHE: All the time I was trying to tell her that I was sorry she had bit my nose, she kept saying that I was someone else. She called me an old fool. (*Pauses*) I wonder who she thought I was. (*Sees* CRISPIN) Ah, ha, what are you doing here?

ANGELICA: It's all right now, Papa. Andre is no longer a suitor. He is leaving the country.

CRISPIN: For his health, I think.

ADOLPHE: Then you have only one suitor?

ANGELICA: Yes, Papa. Crispin is my only suitor! And he suits me fine.

ADOLPHE: Then you may marry. (*Going up and peering into* CRISPIN's *face*) But, do you know something, my son? With my glasses on, I think you look very much like a table I used to know. (*Curtain*)

THE END

THE GATES OF DINKELSBUEHL
(Germany)

Author's Notes on THE GATES OF DINKELSBUEHL

One of the oldest festivals in Germany is the Dinkelsbuehl Kinderzeche (The Children's Festival), which commemorates an incident during the Thirty Years War over three hundred years ago. The Festival itself started about 1635. During the Thirty Years War, three burgomasters of Dinkelsbuehl, Germany, received a warning from the Swedish general demanding that the city surrender. Sweden was at this time one of the strongest military nations of Europe, and the burgomasters knew that if they surrendered, the Swedes would destroy the city. But since Dinkelsbuehl lacked both food and the force to resist, they felt they would have to surrender anyway. Through the courage and imagination of a little girl and the heroism of all the children of Dinkelsbuehl, war was averted and the city was saved. The annual Festival which commemorates this event includes a Children's Band parade, folk dances—both German and Swedish—and singing.

Although the action of this play is both melodramatic and heroic, the play itself—like an Austrian musical comedy—should be light in tone. The action should be treated merely as the occasion for the singing, dancing, and parading.

The Gates of Dinkelsbuehl

Characters

BURGOMASTER SCHMIDT	GENERAL GUSTAVUS ADOLPHUS
BURGOMASTER BRAUN	FIRST SWEDISH CAPTAIN
BURGOMASTER STEIN	SECOND SWEDISH CAPTAIN
BERTHA	THE CHILDREN'S BAND
JOHANN	SWEDISH MESSENGER

SETTING: *The main street of the city of Dinkelsbuehl, before the gates of the city.*

AT RISE: *The* THREE BURGOMASTERS *rush on stage and meet at the intersection of the two streets. They are obviously very excited and very frightened.* SCHMIDT *comes from the gate;* BRAUN *from stage left; and* STEIN *from stage right.*

BRAUN: Are they still there? Are the Swedes still there?

SCHMIDT: They are still there. General Gustavus Adolphus and sixteen thousand of his soldiers. They are a fierce-looking crew.

STEIN: Do they still demand we surrender?

SCHMIDT: It makes no difference to them what we do. When the sun reaches the middle of the sky, they will attack. Our gates, our city walls, will fall.

BRAUN: Is there nothing we can do? Can't we stop them?

SCHMIDT: We don't have three thousand men, women, children and chickens in our whole village. We could not even slow them down.

STEIN: We have no choice. We must surrender.

SCHMIDT: It makes no difference. If we try to stop them, they will destroy Dinkelsbuehl as they enter the city. If we surrender, they will destroy Dinkelsbuehl after they enter the city. It's really a very small choice—a matter of seconds, really.

BRAUN: Perhaps if we asked General Adolphus nicely— pleaded with him, begged him, got down on our knees —perhaps he might spare Dinkelsbuehl. We are only a very small village, and he is a very large general.

STEIN: Maybe we could tell him that it would hurt his reputation. We could explain to him that we are only a miserable, little village . . . hardly more than a shack on the road.

BRAUN: I do not think that would be good for business.

SCHMIDT: It does not make any difference whether we are as great as Berlin or as small as a flea; Dinkelsbuehl stands between him and the Austrians. He does not want a German village at his back as he marches South. He will not listen to us.

BRAUN: Perhaps if we promised him our wealth?

SCHMIDT: He will take it anyway.

STEIN: Perhaps if we gave him our weapons?

SCHMIDT: We have no weapons to give, none of any importance to the great General Adolphus.

STEIN: Then what can we do?

SCHMIDT: We might hold the gates against the first attack, for a few minutes, perhaps, but it would do no good.

BRAUN: If we are going to have to surrender, why don't we do it now? I hate waiting for something to happen.

SCHMIDT: We will wait until noon, just before he attacks, the last possible moment. This is the last day for Dinkelsbuehl. We might as well enjoy it as long as possible. (*Enter* BERTHA, *a shy little girl, from off-stage right.*)

STEIN: I am not enjoying it very much, but there seems to be nothing else to do.

BRAUN: There is nothing that we can do.

SCHMIDT: Nothing. (*All three stand glumly, thinking and sighing.* BERTHA *pulls at* SCHMIDT'S *coat.*)

BERTHA: Burgomaster Schmidt.

SCHMIDT: Go away, little girl. Can't you see we are thinking?

BERTHA: What are we going to do, Burgomaster Schmidt?

SCHMIDT: Listen to that. She wants to know what we are going to do.

BRAUN: I can tell you what we are going to do.

STEIN: It's really very simple.

SCHMIDT: We are going to do nothing because there is nothing we can do. Now go away and leave us alone to think.

BERTHA: I have a plan. I have heard that General Adolphus has received sad news from home.

SCHMIDT: And I have received sad news while at home. Go away.

BRAUN: Perhaps if we offered him money. No, I forgot. We have already thought of that.

BERTHA: General Adolphus has received word that his young son is dead.

STEIN: We know that. What is that to us? Soon we will all be homeless.

BERTHA: But perhaps if you would send some children . . .

BRAUN: Go away, little girl.

STEIN: Don't you hear? Go away.

SCHMIDT: Come, we will never get any planning done here. Burgomaster Braun, go see the merchants and tell them at noon we surrender.

BRAUN (*Turning to leave stage left*): They will not like it, but there is nothing else we can do, nothing, absolutely nothing. (*Exit* BRAUN.)

SCHMIDT: Burgomaster Stein, you see the farmers and tell them the same.

STEIN (*Turning to leave stage right*): They will like it even less than the merchants, but there is nothing we can do. Absolutely nothing. (*Exit* STEIN.)

BERTHA: There is something you can do. I have a plan.

SCHMIDT: Go away, little girl. Go away! No, you stay here, since you seem to like it so well. I'll go away. I wish I could. (*Exit* SCHMIDT.)

BERTHA (*Calling after him*): Burgomaster Schmidt! Burgomaster Schmidt! Please listen to me. I have a plan, a plan! (*Enter* JOHANN *from stage right*.)

JOHANN: Bertha! Bertha!

BERTHA (*Turning toward him*): They would not listen to me, Johann.

JOHANN: I knew they would not. One does not get to be a burgomaster by listening to other people.

BERTHA: They are going to surrender the city at noon. They say there is nothing else we can do.

JOHANN: I guess there is no help for it.

BERTHA: General Adolphus will destroy the city and send us all away from our homes.

JOHANN: That is what happened to the people in the villages near Wurzburg and Mainz. So I guess it will happen to us, too.

BERTHA: It will be a terrible thing to be driven out of our homes.

JOHANN: I will take care of you, little Bertha.

BERTHA: Burgomaster Braun wanted to give the General money.

JOHANN: In war you do not give the winners anything. They take what they want.

BERTHA: But it is not really a war. We have not done anything to the Swedes. I think that if we explained to General Adolphus, he would understand. Especially if we could try my plan.

JOHANN: It would have done no harm to try the plan.

BERTHA: Do you think it would have worked, Johann?

JOHANN: It would have been no worse than no plan.

BERTHA: Would you help me with it?

JOHANN: Do you mean that we should do it ourselves? It would make the burgomasters angry that we took such matters upon ourselves.

BERTHA: I do not care if they are angry. If the plan does not work, their anger cannot hurt us. If it does work, they will have no reason to be angry.

JOHANN: Even if it doesn't work and even if they are angry, I do not care. I will help you, Bertha.

BERTHA: You know what we are to do. (*Points off right*) You go as far as the wall to the west, and I shall go to the wall in the east. Bring all the children you can find, and tell them to bring drums and fifes and horns and whatever else they have. What we lack in size, we must make up for in noise.

JOHANN (*Saluting*): I'll bring them in order, marching like an army of kings, my General.

BERTHA (*Saluting*): And I shall, too. We may not succeed, Johann, but the world will know we tried. (BERTHA *and* JOHANN *run off. Upstage center back of the gate, a bell rings.*)

OFF-STAGE VOICE: Burgomasters of Dinkelsbuehl. Burgomasters of Dinkelsbuehl! (*The* THREE BURGOMASTERS *enter, running.*)

SCHMIDT: Yes, yes. We are coming, mein herr.

BRAUN: One minute, one minute. As fast as our fat, little legs will carry us, we are coming.

STEIN: We are coming, we are coming. Wait! Wait! (*The* THREE BURGOMASTERS *run to the gates and drop to their knees.*)

SCHMIDT: We are here, mein herr.

OFF-STAGE VOICE: Can you hear my voice?

STEIN: Yes, indeed. And a very fine voice it is.

VOICE: In five minutes, the sun will stand high in the sky. Then we will attack your city. If you do not open the gates, we will knock them down. Five minutes, do you hear?

BRAUN: We hear, but we do not like what we hear.

SCHMIDT: If we open the gates for you, will you spare our city?

OFF-STAGE VOICE: We do not care whether or not you open the gates. It is all the same to us whether we walk through them or over them.

STEIN: It would be much easier to walk through them.

You would not have to dirty your hands knocking them down.

BRAUN: Yes, yes. You might even tear your trousers if you had to walk over them.

OFF-STAGE VOICE: We have not come to bargain. We have come to conquer. You have five minutes. Then we attack. (*The* THREE BURGOMASTERS *rise.*)

SCHMIDT: I have worked a whole lifetime, and now I will lose everything. I must go home and hide grandfather's picture. I should not want the Swedes to get that. (*He runs off.*)

STEIN: Everything will be lost: the pork in the barrels, the silks in the closet, and my gold. I must run home and hide . . . and hide grandmother's picture. I certainly do not want the Swedes to get that. (*He runs off.*)

BRAUN: Schmidt and Stein never had a grandfather or a grandmother, and if they had, they certainly would not care what happened to their pictures. They are going to hide their money. Fine leaders they are, to be thinking only of money at a time like this. Money! The Swedes will find MY money. I must run home and hide it. (*He runs off. The stage remains empty for a few seconds; then the sounds of drums and whistles are heard. Coming from both stage right and left, the Children's Band enters, one group led by* BERTHA *and the other by* JOHANN. *They march two-at-a-time until they meet at the downstage end of the street leading to the gates; then they join in groups of four and march to the gate. After this marching episode is completed, the children stand facing center stage, and flanking the gates, in a military formation.* BERTHA *and* JOHANN *stand away from the groups, in front of the gates.*)

BERTHA: Here we are, Johann. Are you afraid?

JOHANN: Open the gates, Bertha. We are ready to face the enemy.

BERTHA: I thought maybe you would open them, Johann. You are a boy.

JOHANN: But it was your idea, and you are the general. I am only your captain.

BERTHA: But if General Adolphus saw I was only a girl, he might be angry.

JOHANN (*Laughing*): We shall open them together. Now stand straight, General Bertha. We must never let an enemy see that we are afraid. (*They march to the gates and open them, while the* DRUMMERS *in the Children's Band beat time. When the gates are opened,* GENERAL ADOLPHUS *and two of his* CAPTAINS *march in. They have their swords drawn, but when they see only* CHILDREN, *they stop amazed.*)

FIRST CAPTAIN: What is this? A village with nothing but children.

ADOLPHUS (*Letting his sword drop down*): I had forgotten that behind every city wall there are so many children.

SECOND CAPTAIN: This is the youngest army we have ever faced, General. But very fierce-looking, aren't they?

ADOLPHUS (*To* BERTHA *and* JOHANN): And who is in command of this army?

JOHANN: She is, sir. (*Points to* BERTHA.) She is the general. I am her captain.

FIRST CAPTAIN: We'd better be careful, General. She has the look of another Joan of Arc.

ADOLPHUS: Are you another Joan of Arc, General?

BERTHA: I am not really a general, sir, and this is not really an army, and I have never heard of Joan of Arc.

SECOND CAPTAIN: Never heard of Joan of Arc? Why she is famous everywhere!

FIRST CHILD: She's not Joan of Arc. She's Bertha. Everybody knows that.

SECOND CHILD: But she's famous everywhere in our village.

THIRD CHILD: Everybody in Dinkelsbuehl knows Bertha because she is the child who never says anything.

ADOLPHUS: A general who never says anything? Now that is an odd one. How do you give orders?

JOHANN: She gives the orders to me, sir.

ADOLPHUS: And you?

JOHANN: I obey, sir.

ADOLPHUS: Now has she given you orders to attack our army and drive us away?

JOHANN: No, sir.

ADOLPHUS: But if she does, will you obey?

JOHANN: I will try, sir.

ADOLPHUS (*To* FIRST CAPTAIN): He looks very much like my son, does he not, Captain?

FIRST CAPTAIN: Very much, General. But perhaps not so large in the shoulders as was young Prince Carl.

BERTHA: We did not come to fight against your army, sir.

ADOLPHUS: Is this then a surrender?

BERTHA: We came to . . . to . . . .

ADOLPHUS: To what, child?

BERTHA: To offer a trade.

ADOLPHUS: A trade?

BERTHA: We have heard that your only child has died, sir.

ADOLPHUS: I am listening.

BERTHA: Is it true, sir?

ADOLPHUS (*Getting angry*): What is it to you! (*Then softer*) Yes, it is true. My only son, my only child, Carl, is dead.

BERTHA: We came to tell you that we are very sorry that you have lost your child.

ADOLPHUS: Did the burgomasters send you?

JOHANN: They would not even listen to her plan.

ADOLPHUS: A plan! What plan do you have?

FIRST CAPTAIN: Perhaps it is some sort of a trick, General.

SECOND CAPTAIN: While we are standing here talking to these children, their army may be circling behind us.

BERTHA: We have no army.

JOHANN: It isn't that kind of a plan. We have no tricks.

ADOLPHUS: Well, Little General Who Never Speaks, it is time you said something.

BERTHA: It is a terrible thing for a father to lose a child, to go home where a child was and find no child there. If you will spare our city, one of us will be your child.

ADOLPHUS: What! Anyone I choose?

BERTHA: Yes, sir.

ADOLPHUS: If I choose Johann here, he will be my son?

JOHANN: Yes, sir.

ADOLPHUS: And if I choose you, Bertha, will you be my son?

JOHANN: She is only a girl, sir.

ADOLPHUS: I shall raise her as a boy. I shall teach her to be a soldier and to ride at my side in battle. Would you like that, Bertha?

BERTHA: If you wish, sir.

ADOLPHUS: And you will not miss your mother and father?

BERTHA: I shall never cry where anyone can see me. I shall be the best son I can for you.

JOHANN: Why not take me, General? I am already a son, so it should not be so hard.

ADOLPHUS: No. I shall take Bertha.

BERTHA: Yes, sir. I am ready to go when you wish me.

ADOLPHUS: And when you are far away from your home, cold on the march, hungry, a single child among rough soldiers, shall you not regret that you made this choice?

BERTHA: I shall be a good son to you, General.

ADOLPHUS: (*Laughing*): I am sure you would, Bertha. I am sure you would, and I shall take you with me in my heart. Whenever I am sad because I have no child of my own, I shall think of you. Then perhaps I shall not be so sad. You may stay in your city. The Gates of Dinkelsbuehl shall remain standing.

JOHANN: You will spare our city, General?

ADOLPHUS: Yes, Captain, I shall spare your city. I met your general in fair combat, and she won. (*To the* FIRST CAPTAIN) Captain, give orders to the troops that we march in an hour. With an ally like General Bertha in the city, it will be all right to have it at our backs.

FIRST CAPTAIN: Yes, sir, we shall be ready to leave in an hour. (*Exit* CAPTAIN *through gates.*)

ADOLPHUS: And, Little General, you are a Joan of Arc after all. You have saved your city. (*Enter the* THREE BURGOMASTERS *running, one following upon the heels of another, and all very excited.*)

SCHMIDT: The gates are open.

BRAUN: The enemy is within.

STEIN: We have been betrayed. Oh, my poor grandmother's picture.

ADOLPHUS: These, I should judge, are the burgomasters, come to save the day.

SECOND CAPTAIN: They look more like the three blind mice.

SCHMIDT (*Almost falling at* ADOLPHUS' *feet*): General Adolphus, welcome to our city.

STEIN: We intended to be here to welcome you.

BRAUN: At noon, we were going to open the gates.

SCHMIDT: We surrender. You do not have to fight.

STEIN: Indeed not. We surrender.

BRAUN: It is the only thing we can do.

ADOLPHUS: Be quiet. You do not need to surrender. We have met your strongest force, and you have won. Your city is spared.

STEIN: Our strongest force?

ADOLPHUS: This child, Bertha, these children.

SCHMIDT: Bertha? Bertha saved the city?

BRAUN: I knew we should have listened to her.

SCHMIDT: You! You told her to go away. I was the last one to talk to her.

STEIN: You told her to go away. I have been a friend of her father for twenty years. I knew we should have listened to her.

ADOLPHUS: Will you be quiet! My army leaves in an hour. I shall require only water.

SCHMIDT: You shall have all the water you need.

STEIN: We would even give you milk, if we had it.

BRAUN: And cheese, if we had it.

SCHMIDT: But we have nothing but water. Our gates have been closed to commerce for many weeks now.

ADOLPHUS: I require only water for the horses and men.

SCHMIDT: Certainly, General. Would you and your officers care to rest while we take the water to your camp?

BERTHA: We have some dances and music for you, if you think that you would care to see us dance, General?

ADOLPHUS: That would be very nice, Child. But . . .

SCHMIDT (*Breaking in*): Of course, General, we understand. (*To* BERTHA) Now that you children have done your good deed, why don't you go home?

ADOLPHUS: No, let this be the children's day. Let this day be set aside for them, yes, for their children and their children's children, a day for children to celebrate a child's victory over war. I think I *would* like to see children dance now.

BERTHA: We shall be pleased. And we have a surprise for you—a Swedish folk dance. (*The children form into a group, and dance a Swedish folk dance.*)

ADOLPHUS (*To* CAPTAIN): I may have made a mistake, Captain. With General Bertha at my side, Sweden would have ruled all of Europe. (*The dance ends and the curtain falls.*)

THE END

THE SKILL OF PERICLES

(*Greece*)

Pericles, a fifth-century B.C. Athenian statesman, is, like our own Thomas Jefferson, one of the great heroes of democracy. Under his guidance, Athens became the great hope of free men; and it is a tribute to the soundness of the democratic idea that Athens also became the leader in many other areas of human endeavor: physical development, art, drama, poetry, commerce, oratory, and science.

The Greek leaders of the age of Pericles made such great contributions to democracy and the advance of civilization that they are called the "fathers of western civilization," and the time in which they lived is known as "The Golden Age of Athens." But of all the accomplishments of the period, what pleased Pericles most was that no man was made to suffer to achieve the general progress. The "skill" of Pericles is the understanding that a nation prospers best when each man is encouraged to do his best in that activity which pleases him most.

While the greatest virtue of a democratic society is respect for others, at the same time, the theatrical effectiveness of this play depends upon the excellence of the individual "routines." If a talent not included in this play is possessed by one of the actors, the director should change the business to give that actor a chance to display his individual talent.

The Skill of Pericles

Characters

CIMON (*The Athlete*)   NESTOR (*The Friend*)
HECTOR (*The Orator*)   THE OLD SAILOR
AJAX (*The Warrior*)   A MESSENGER
HELENA (*The Beauty*)   PERICLES
LETA (*The Wise*)   CITIZENS OF ATHENS
IDA (*The Artful*)

TIME: *The fifth century,* B.C.

SETTING: *The market place in Athens.*

AT RISE: *The* OLD SAILOR *is telling a story about the voyages he has taken. The* SAILOR *and the young people—*CIMON, HECTOR, AJAX, HELENA, LETA, IDA, *and* NESTOR—*are downstage left and hold the center of attention, but the* CITIZENS *of Athens can be seen carrying on their business upstage. The* OLD SAILOR *pretends his tales are true; actually he takes them from the stories of Homer, "The Iliad" and "The Odyssey," but he is very interesting and a favorite with the young people.*

THE SAILOR: And there we were—Odysseus and I—and there was the great big Cyclops. . . .

CIMON: Was the Cyclops as big as ten men?

THE SAILOR: As big as fifty and he had one eye (*Points to the middle of his forehead*) right in the middle of his forehead.

CIMON: I'll bet he could run like the wind.

AJAX: And fight like an army.

HELENA: But he wasn't very pretty.

THE SAILOR: He was ugly all right, and he would have scared any other man to death—except my friend Odysseus and me.

LETA (*Doubting*): How could you know Odysseus? He lived a long time ago.

THE SAILOR: That's a fact. A long time ago. But I was younger then.

LETA: I thought it was *a thousand years ago*.

THE SAILOR: It may have been. I was a lot younger then.

IDA: Did Homer tell the truth about Odysseus, old sailor?

THE SAILOR: He was a poet and all poets make up stories. But mostly he told the truth.

LETA: Why didn't he mention you?

THE SAILOR: Well, I guess Homer couldn't write down everything.

HELENA: Tell us about your adventures with our leader, Pericles.

THE SAILOR: Ah, yes, Pericles and I.

LETA: Huh. I'll bet you were never at Troy and you probably don't even know Pericles.

THE SAILOR: Pericles and I have done some big things.

LETA: You made up those stories about Pericles.

NESTOR: What do you want to say that for, Leta? Now he won't tell us any more stories.

LETA: I said it because it's true.

THE SAILOR: Is that so, young girl? Maybe you would believe me if I brought Pericles here and he told you himself?

LETA: Yes, I would. Bring him if you can.

THE SAILOR: Maybe I just don't want to bring him.

LETA: You wouldn't know Pericles even if you saw him. (*A* MESSENGER *enters upstage center and hits a brass gong. All the people stop their business to listen to him.*)

MESSENGER (*Unrolling a scroll and reading it*): Hear ye, hear ye, hear ye. I bring news from our great leader, Pericles. Today Pericles will visit you to pick the youth who best shows he knows the skill of Pericles.

FIRST CITIZEN: The skill of Pericles? What's that?

SECOND CITIZEN: His military skill, of course.

THIRD CITIZEN: Not so. It's his speech-making.

FOURTH CITIZEN: It's his strength.

MESSENGER (*Hitting gong again to silence crowd*): Pericles is already among you, looking and judging. Within the hour he shall say who best has the skill of Pericles. Parents, prepare your children. Children, be prepared. The one chosen shall win a prize. (MESSENGER *exits.*)

FIRST CITIZEN: Pericles is already among us, judging.

SECOND CITIZEN: Within the hour he will name the winner.

THIRD CITIZEN: I must go home and rouse my lazy son from sleep. But what's the use? Only if sleeping is the skill of Pericles will he win the prize.

FOURTH CITIZEN: Perhaps it is singing. My little girl has the voice of a bird.

FIFTH CITIZEN (*To* 4TH CITIZEN): The voice of a bird all right—a crow. Your daughter cannot sing.

FOURTH CITIZEN: You are jealous. You know it will bring great honor to my house if my child wins the prize. (*During the past several speeches, the* CITIZENS *have been leaving. Now only the seven main characters are left onstage. Upstage center* PERICLES, *disguised as a beggar, sits with his head bent, as though he were half-asleep.*)

CIMON: What is this skill of Pericles? Did anyone ever say?

HELENA: I have never heard of such a thing before.

NESTOR: Wouldn't it be a great honor if one of you should win the prize? I would be very proud to have a friend who has the skill of Pericles.

HECTOR: The old sailor said he knew Pericles well. The sailor can tell us. Where is he?

IDA (*Looking about*): He's gone. Leta made him angry when she said he made up stories.

LETA: I didn't make him angry. He knew that when Pericles came, we would find out his stories were not true.

AJAX: If you think he makes things up, why do you listen to him?

LETA: He tells very good stories. (PERICLES *now comes downstage and joins the group. They pay no attention to him.*)

CIMON: We Greeks are the finest athletes in all the world. We run the fastest, swim the best, hurl the javelin farther than any other people on earth. The skill of Pericles must be in our sports. Nestor, come and race me to the temple and back. If Pericles is watching he will see what a fine runner I am.

NESTOR: Gladly, my friend Cimon, if you think my running with you will help.

CIMON: Hector, tell us when to start.

HECTOR: I don't see why I should help you, Cimon. I, too, would like to win the prize.

NESTOR: Hector, if the prize is for speaking, Pericles will hear your fine voice.

HECTOR: I hadn't thought of that. All right. (CIMON and NESTOR *get in a starting position.*) Great runners of Athens, hear my command: Get ready, set, and go! (*The two run off.*) Didn't my voice sound well, Leta?

LETA: Don't be foolish, Hector. How can a voice sound well unless it says something?

HELENA (*Looking off*): Nestor is almost keeping up with Cimon.

LETA: Nestor is a fine runner, too, but he is more interested in making Cimon a better runner than in winning the race for himself. He will lose.

HELENA: I'm afraid so. And Nestor is nicer than Cimon, too. (NESTOR *and* CIMON *return,* CIMON *leading the race.* HECTOR *takes* CIMON's *hand and raises it.*)

HECTOR: I, Hector, judge: Cimon is the winner.

HELENA: Nestor, you might win a race if you would think about winning instead of trying to make Cimon run faster.

NESTOR: No one can beat my friend Cimon. He is the finest runner in Athens.

CIMON: But you are a great help to me, Nestor. Perhaps Pericles will give a second prize, and you will get it.

HECTOR: You are very quick to take first prize for yourself, Cimon. But I do not think the skill of Pericles is running. Pericles was a great runner in his youth, to be sure. But it takes speaking skill to win men to democracy, not running.

AJAX: Do you think you will win the prize for your speaking, Hector?

HECTOR: I don't say I will win the prize, but I would like to try. Do you remember the story of Admetus, who asked his father to die in his place? Hear me give the father's answer. . . .

LETA (*Breaking in*): Do we have to listen to that speech again?

HECTOR: Hear me, now. I am the old father speaking. (*Pretending to be an old man*) "Am I slave, son, that you treat me so? Or am I your father, a king and a freeman born? I have given you everything you own. Is it my duty to die for you as well? There is no law of the Greeks that a father must die for his son. . . ."

IDA (*Interrupting*): Are you going to give the whole speech again?

NESTOR: I think that is a good speech, and Hector gives it very well.

LETA: I don't know what we would do without you, Nestor. You make all our faults sound like virtues: Cimon's bragging and Hector's bellowing, Ajax's prancing about. . . .

AJAX: I do not prance! I walk like a warrior. And that's what I am, a warrior. You will be sorry you have said that, Leta, when I win the prize.

LETA: Do you think you have the skill of Pericles?

AJAX: What is the greatest skill of the Greeks, I ask you? It is fighting! And who is the greatest warrior here? (*He draws his wooden sword and makes a fake thrust*

toward NESTOR *who pretends to fall dead.*) You see?
Victory again. (*He pretends to place a foot on* NESTOR'S
body and holds his sword aloft.) If Pericles has seen
what a great warrior I am, I am sure to win the prize.

NESTOR (*Getting to his feet again*): One of you will win.
I am sure of it. No one runs as fast as Cimon, or talks
as well as Hector or fights as well as Ajax. We must all
have a feast when the prize is given.

PERICLES (*All turn to him as he speaks*): There is much
in what you say, Nestor. We Greeks prize the gifts of
your friends here. One of them may well win the prize.

NESTOR: I wish Pericles were here saying that.

IDA: Do you know Pericles, old man?

PERICLES: I have never seen him face to face, but I know
something of the way he thinks. (*Turning to girls*)
What about you girls? Helena, here, has beauty. Maybe
that is the skill of Pericles.

HELENA (*Posing*): *I* thought beauty should be the skill
of Pericles, but I did not know men would agree with
me.

PERICLES: We Athenians are not brutes like the Spartans,
Helena. It is our greatness that we know beauty makes
life worth living.

HELENA: If I win the prize, I hope it is a lovely necklace
for my beautiful neck.

LETA: Do not count the beads until you have won the
prize. The Goddess of Beauty won a prize from Paris,
but foolish Paris was not as wise as Pericles. I do not
think a pretty face will be the skill of Pericles.

PERICLES: That is a good argument for one so young.
You are wise, Leta.

NESTOR: Perhaps wisdom is the skill of Pericles, Leta, and then you will win the prize.

LETA: Thank you, Nestor. I am wise enough to know I won't win. All nations have wise people, but all cities are not Athens. I don't know the skill of Pericles, but I do not think it is wisdom.

PERICLES: Perhaps it is art. I am told, Ida, that you sing and dance most wonderfully.

NESTOR: She is the finest singer and dancer in all Athens. Sing for us, Ida.

PERICLES: Yes, do, Ida. We Greeks prize our singers. Think of the honor that we have given our poet Homer these many centuries.

IDA: I'll sing if you all join in.

NESTOR: We will join in your singing and in your dancing too. (*The following song is to be sung to the tune of Bach's "A Song of Praise."* * IDA *sings the first verse alone. The others join her in the second verse. Then* IDA *and* NESTOR *do a ballet routine while the others sing the first verse again.*)

IDA:

> We raise a song to isles we love,
> For all the joys that life does bring:
> For freemen's rights and heroes' deeds,
> Our grateful thanks and praise we sing.

---

* A simple version of "A Song of Praise" may be found on page 76 of *New Music Horizons* (Book 2), published by Silver Burdett Co., 1948. Any traditional Greek song may be used here, such as "The Sponge Diver," on page 170 of *Music in Our Country*, (Book 5), published by Silver Burdett Co., 1957.

OTHERS:

> We raise a song to isles we love,
> For Athens, city that we prize,
> For shining seas and mountains tall,
> In grateful thanks our voices rise.

PERICLES (*Applauding*): That was very good, Ida. And you did well, too, Nestor.

IDA: Nestor is my favorite partner.

NESTOR: Anyone can dance well with Ida.

PERICLES: But what is your special skill, Nestor? How do you expect to win the prize from Pericles?

NESTOR (*Laughing*): I will not even be considered. I do not run as well as Cimon, nor talk as well as Hector. I do not fight as well as Ajax. . . .

AJAX: But you are the one I would want at my side in battle.

NESTOR: I thank you for that, Ajax.

HELENA: You are not beautiful, Nestor. But I think you are handsome. Don't you think so, old man?

PERICLES: He has a good face, one I would like in a son or friend.

NESTOR (*Laughing*): My only skill is the luck to have such good friends. And one of them will win the prize today. I am sure of it. (MESSENGER *enters and strikes the gong again. The* CITIZENS *come onstage again.*)

PERICLES: Well, we shall soon see. Here is the messenger again. (*He leaves the group and goes upstage to the* MESSENGER.)

MESSENGER: Citizens of Greece, the time has come to

announce the name of the youth with the skill of Pericles.

FIRST CITIZEN: But where is Pericles?

SECOND CITIZEN: We have not seen Pericles yet.

THIRD CITIZEN: He has not heard my lazy son snore.

FOURTH CITIZEN: He has not yet heard my little girl sing.

MESSENGER: Pericles has been with you. He has watched you work and play.

AJAX: Pericles has been here? (*The* OLD SAILOR *comes onstage.*)

HELENA: Look, the old sailor! He's back.

MESSENGER: Pericles has been here, and he is here. He has come disguised. But now he will speak.

IDA: Pericles is here disguised.

CIMON: I'll bet the old sailor is Pericles.

HECTOR: You will not win, Leta, because you said he made up stories.

AJAX: The old sailor said he knew Pericles, and surely a man knows himself. (PERICLES *now steps up beside the* MESSENGER.)

LETA: Look! The old beggar is standing next to the messenger. It is not the old sailor, but the old beggar who is Pericles in disguise.

HECTOR: It can't be. He said he had never seen Pericles face to face.

LETA: No man ever sees himself face to face.

MESSENGER: Citizens of Athens! Pericles! (PERICLES *drops the ragged cloak he has had about him, removes the hood from his head, and stands erect.*)

CITIZENS: Pericles! It is Pericles.

FIRST CITIZEN: I have seen him talking to the children by the river's edge.

SECOND CITIZEN: I have seen him listening to the children sing.

THIRD CITIZEN: He has heard my lazy son snore.

FOURTH CITIZEN (*Pleased*): He has heard my little girl sing.

PERICLES: Citizens of Athens, I have come disguised not to trick you, but because I wanted to know you as you know each other—as friend knows friend and fellow-citizen knows fellow-citizen.

FIFTH CITIZEN: That is the democratic way.

PERICLES: I have watched and been pleased. Here are many youths with skills and gifts that make life good.

NESTOR (*To his friends*): You see! He is going to give one of you the prize.

PERICLES: I have seen Cimon race. He will win many palms in the games.

NESTOR: You see, Cimon. He knows.

PERICLES: I have heard Hector speak and seen Ajax fight. With such voices and willing hearts, Athens will long remain free.

NESTOR: Perhaps he will give three prizes.

PERICLES: And I have seen Helena's beautiful face and Ida's grace, and I have heard the wise words of Leta. All our poets will sing of these three.

NESTOR: He's going to give six prizes!

PERICLES: And there are other youths, too. Jason, who works with his father in the olive groves, and Hymen who sails a boat so well across the waters. Each has skills I wish I had. But my only skill is in knowing that all men have skills.

FIRST CITIZEN: That is true. He knows men have skills that they do not know they have.

PERICLES: Now which youth among you best knows your virtues? What say you, Cimon?

CIMON: My friend, Nestor.

PERICLES: What say you, Hector?

HECTOR: My friend, Nestor.

PERICLES: What say you, Ajax?

AJAX: My friend, Nestor.

PERICLES: What say you, Citizens of Athens?

ALL: Our friend, Nestor.

FIRST CITIZEN: He listens to me when I am sad.

SECOND CITIZEN: He sings with me when I am happy.

THIRD CITIZEN: He is happy when I am fortunate.

PERICLES: Then, my friends, *your* choice is Nestor. He is our friend, and before the sun sets, we will honor him today as he honors us every day of his life. Go to your homes to prepare, and return before the sun sets. (*All except the* OLD SAILOR, PERICLES, *and the seven young people depart, speaking as they go.*)

FIRST CITIZEN: It was a good choice.

SECOND CITIZEN: He has always been a friend to all.

THIRD CITIZEN: And he says my son is not lazy, just thinking, and one day he will be a fine man.

FOURTH CITIZEN: He loves to hear my little girl sing. (*All exit.*)

PERICLES (*Who has made his way down to the seven*): Well, my young friends, I know you all agree, but what did you learn from this?

LETA: Something we should have known: the first prize in a democracy goes to those who give, not to those who have.

PERICLES: You are wise, Leta, and if you have the wisdom to comfort people, you will be honored all the days of your life. (*The* OLD SAILOR *attempts to move offstage without being noticed.* PERICLES *shouts to him.*) Wait a minute, old sailor, my friend. (*To the others*) I must go see my old friend, the sailor. He fought alongside me in many a battle. I must seek his advice on how to make our country better. (*As he is leaving.*) He was with Odysseus when they escaped from the Cyclops, you know. (*He goes to the* OLD SAILOR *and they exit together.*)

CIMON: Did you hear, Leta? The old sailor *was* with Odysseus. You were wrong.

AJAX: You said that he did not even know Pericles. And now you have seen what great friends they are.

LETA: They are now. That is Pericles' skill, to use one's gift to help others. I don't know if the old sailor ever saw Pericles before, but he will never forget him now. (*Curtain*)

THE END

A LEAK IN THE DIKE

(Holland)

Author's Notes on A LEAK IN THE DIKE

In 1865, Mary Mapes Dodge wrote *Hans Brinker: Or the Silver Skates*. What is now best remembered about this ever-popular book is not the main story of the silver skates at all, but a short, three-page anecdote which Miss Dodge invented as a school lesson, "The Hero of Haarlem." There was apparently no basis in history for this story, but so well did it typify Dutch courage that the Hollanders soon accepted the story as a symbol of their eternal struggle against the sea.

The main episode of *A Leak in the Dike* is based on this anecdote in *Hans Brinker,* with some alterations for dramatic purposes. As Miss Dodge herself writes of "The Hero of Haarlem," "That little boy represents the spirit of the whole country. Not a leak can show itself anywhere, either in politics, honor, or public safety, that a million fingers are not ready to stop, at any cost."

A Leak in the Dike

Characters

GRANDFATHER
GRANDDAUGHTER
JAN VAN HOOF, *the hero of Haarlem*
NETTY
VINCENT
JULIANA
ADRIAN HAAS, *the bovenmeester* (*school master*)
BOREIN APELDOORN

TIME: *Late afternoon.*
SETTING: *The base of the dike in Haarlem, bordered with tulips.*
AT RISE: GRANDFATHER *and* GRANDDAUGHTER *enter from left. The little girl is skipping and singing.*

GRANDDAUGHTER (*Singing to tune of "Yankee Doodle"*):

> Yanker didee, dudel down
> Didee dudel lawnter
> Yanker viver, voyer vown,
> Botwemelk und Tawnter.

(*She stops as she sees the tulips, and runs to them.*)
Look, Grandfather, tulips. Aren't they pretty?

GRANDFATHER: The prettiest in the world, my child.

GRANDDAUGHTER: See how straight they stand.

GRANDFATHER: Everything Dutch stands straight, my child. And our tulips should do no less.

GRANDDAUGHTER: Don't all tulips stand straight, Grandfather? Even English tulips and French tulips?

GRANDFATHER: Yes, but that's because all the tulips of the world first came from Holland. But even so, they don't stand so straight in other lands as here.

GRANDDAUGHTER: Is that really true, Grandfather?

GRANDFATHER (*Laughs*): I like to think it is true. Every year when we ship our tulips all over the world, I like to think they droop a little in other lands because they are homesick for the Dutch soil.

GRANDDAUGHTER: Grandfather, you are fooling me. I don't think flowers even know what soil they are on.

GRANDFATHER (*Bending over and picking up a handful of earth*): Everything that ever lived or grew in Holland knows Dutch soil. It's a special kind of earth. It was won with a special kind of work and love.

GRANDDAUGHTER: You mean because we took it from the sea, Grandfather?

GRANDFATHER: Because we took it, and because we hold it. (*He pats the side of the dike.*) We and our good dikes.

GRANDDAUGHTER: You love these old dikes, don't you, Grandfather?

GRANDFATHER: Like a bird loves his wings. And for the same reason: they keep us free.

GRANDDAUGHTER: Tell me again about the time the dike broke, Grandfather.

GRANDFATHER: I have told you a thousand times, but all

right. Somewhere a little leak started, and the sea seeped in, then the leak became a hole, then the hole became a gateway. And the sea rushed in. And soon our land was covered.

GRANDDAUGHTER: All from just a little leak, Grandfather?

GRANDFATHER: All from just a little leak. It's like a little hole in a balloon, and the sea is like the air in the balloon. But come. Your mother is waiting for us, and if we are late for our supper, she will not let us go walking tomorrow.

GRANDDAUGHTER: All right, Grandfather. (*She starts skipping and singing, "Yanker Didee, dudel down," and exits.*)

GRANDFATHER (*Patting the dike*): Old Friend, stand guard and keep the North Sea out of our beds tonight. (*Exits after* GRANDDAUGHTER. JAN *and* NETTY *enter from left. He carries a book which he is reading. She carries a basket, covered with a white napkin.*)

NETTY (*Sees the tulips and rushes to them*): Look, Jan, the tulips are in bloom.

JAN (*Without looking up*): Of course. Tulips are always in bloom in April.

NETTY: You must have read that in your book, for you never take your head out of it to look at anything.

JAN (*Looking up*): Are you angry with me, Netty?

NETTY: No, I am not angry with you, Jan van Hoof, but it is not very pleasant to walk along with a person with his head in a book all the time.

JAN: I am sorry, Netty. I did not think. But books have such wonderful things in them, that every time I see a new book it is like seeing a window that looks into a land one has never visited.

NETTY: There are many wonderful things outside books, too, you know.

JAN: That's true, but they are even more wonderful after you see them in a book. Take this old dike, for example. You can just look at it, and all you can see is a stone wall. But then you read about it, and you see the thousands of people who have worked for hundreds of years to build it and keep it in repair. And you see the sea beyond the wall, and you see the days of the past—bad days when the sea broke through the wall. And good days when the dikes were rebuilt. And it all becomes much more exciting.

NETTY: But you don't see the dike that is here, just the one in the book. You don't look at life—just at books.

JAN: I see the dike here! See, I am looking at it!

NETTY: You don't even see what is right beneath your nose. Look, there is a little leak, and you didn't even see it.

JAN (*Excited*): What? Where? It can't be. Do not joke about such things.

NETTY: I am not joking. There is a leak! Right here. (*She points to a place in the dike near the ground.*) You see! All the time you tell me about how wonderful the dikes of Holland are, and here right in front of you there is one with a leak, and you did not even see it.

JAN (*Looking at leak*): We have to find something to stop this leak, Netty.

NETTY: It is only a little leak. It can do no harm.

JAN: It is only a little leak now. In an hour it will be a hole. In two hours it will be a river.

NETTY: From such a little trickle? I don't believe it. Why,

the hole is so small, you could plug it with your finger.

JAN (*Looking closely, and putting his finger in the hole in the dike*): Yes, it just fits. But it is cold. Netty, run quickly and bring someone to fix the hole. I will hold my finger here until you return.

NETTY: I don't know if I can. I must take this food to Aunt Mecka in Haarlem. She is ill, and there is no one to care for her.

JAN: You can take the food later. This is important, Netty.

NETTY: I am already late now, and if I do not hurry, it will be dark before I get there.

JAN: It doesn't matter. You must find someone to come and fix the leak.

NETTY: It does too matter! My mother would not like me to be out alone after dark.

JAN: Netty, listen to me. This is serious. If this leak is not stopped, the whole city may awaken tomorrow and find itself under the sea.

NETTY: Well—I don't know. *Somebody* else will come. My mother would never let me go to my aunt's again if I did not get there by dark.

JAN: She will understand.

NETTY: She will understand that I didn't get there.

JAN: Please, Netty, you must get someone.

NETTY: Well, I'll try. But if I don't come back, you'll know I didn't see anyone. (*She exits right, running.*)

JAN (*Yelling after her*): You have to see someone! Hurry, I can feel the water around my finger. (*He sits down and tries to get comfortable, holding his finger in the dike all the while.*) Oh, this water is cold, and I think my finger is swelling. All the better to plug the leak, I guess. (*The stage lights begin to dim very slowly.*)

What if Netty doesn't find anyone? What can I do? (*He sits quietly for a few seconds, and then he starts to sing quietly and rather tunelessly.*) "Yanker didee, dudel down, Didee dudel lawnter . . ." The leak seems to be getting larger. (*Yells*) Help! Help! Somebody come. The dike has a leak. Help! Help! (*He waits a moment.*) I'd better save my strength. I must stay awake. I'll sing some more. "*Yanker didee, dudel down . . .*" Won't somebody come? Please, somebody, come! (*The curtain falls or the lights go out, to indicate the passage of time. When the scene is revealed again, the stage is in moonlight, and* JAN *appears to be asleep, leaning against the dike. He straightens up suddenly.*) Have I been asleep? The leak! It seems larger, but no water is coming through. Where is Netty? Why doesn't she come? It is so cold here. I wish that I had worn more clothes. (*He awkwardly tries to get more comfortable.*) I am stiff all over, and my finger aches like a toothache. Maybe I could take my finger out and run and get help before anything happens. No, I'd better not try. Anyway, my finger is so swollen that it probably wouldn't come out easily. (*Yells*) Help! Help! Doesn't anyone hear me? Doesn't anyone hear me? (VINCENT *and* JULIANA *come creeping in, holding hands, and looking frightened.*)

VINCENT: Jan! Jan van Hoof, are you here?

JULIANA: He's not here! I told you he wouldn't be. That Netty is always making things up. He is home asleep.

JAN: Help! Help! Over here!

VINCENT: There he is. Over there. (*They run to him.*)

JAN: Why did you take so long to come? My legs are so

stiff from the cold, I shall not be able to walk. Have you brought someone to fix the leak?

VINCENT: We would have come sooner—

JULIANA: But at first we did not believe Netty.

VINCENT: And then we were afraid to tell anyone, for fear that if Netty were making a joke, she would get into trouble. And then we had to wait until everyone went to sleep so that we could sneak out. Is there really a leak, Jan?

JAN: Yes, here. See—I have my finger in it. I think it is getting a little larger, but it is all right now that you are here.

JULIANA: What should we do?

JAN: Go and bring someone to fix the leak. And do it quickly.

VINCENT: Whom should we bring? I would not want to wake my father.

JAN: Just bring anyone: Van Deiper, the gatekeeper, or Bovenmeester Haas, or your uncle, or anyone. But please hurry. I ache and I am cold all over, and the sea is pushing against this hole so that I am not sure how much longer my finger can hold the water back.

VINCENT: I shall go right away.

JULIANA: Wait a minute, Vincent. We *can't* go now.

VINCENT: Why not?

JULIANA: How will we explain that we have sneaked out of our beds at four o'clock in the morning?

VINCENT: I hadn't thought of that.

JULIANA: You know what Mother and Father would say.

JAN: Listen to me, both of you. There is no time to worry about what may happen to us. If help does not come soon, the whole dike may crack and the North Sea come in.

JULIANA: Well, I guess you're right, but I just know we are going to get into trouble.

VINCENT: Can't you wait just a little longer, Jan? It will be morning soon, and then we can bring help.

JAN: I can wait if I have to. But will the North Sea wait? Look, already a few drops are starting to get past my finger.

JULIANA (*Bending over and looking closely*): It is starting to seep in. And your finger looks so strange. Does it hurt, Jan?

JAN: I don't feel anything in it now, but I can't move it. It is just stiff, I guess. But will you please go for help? Even now it may be too late.

JULIANA: Yes, we'll go.

VINCENT: Who will hear us knocking on the door at this hour of the morning?

JULIANA: I will go to Borein Apeldoorn's house. She gets up very early to milk the cows. She is very old and wise, and she will know what to do.

VINCENT: I shall go to the schoolmaster's house. Sometimes Bovenmeester Haas sits up all night looking in his books. He may still be awake. (VINCENT *runs off right, and* JULIANA *left.*)

JAN: But hurry! Hurry! (*Curtain or blackout. When the scene is revealed again, it is early morning.* JAN *now has finger in the dike, while his other hand is pressed around the finger to try to hold back the water that is seeping through.* GRANDFATHER *and* GRANDDAUGHTER *come in.*)

GRANDDAUGHTER: Grandfather, look at that little boy. What a funny place to sit.

GRANDFATHER: Why, it is young Jan van Hoof. (*Going to him*) What are you doing there, boy?

JAN: Thank heavens you've come by. There is a leak in the dike, and I am trying to hold the water back.

GRANDFATHER: A leak in the dike! Good heavens, let me see. (*He bends over and looks.*) Yes. Yes, I see. And there is water coming in. But your finger! What has happened to it?

JAN: I don't know, sir. It's stopped feeling.

GRANDFATHER: Stopped feeling? How long have you been here?

JAN: Since last evening. It's been only one night, but it seems like a whole lifetime ago. (JULIANA *enters, leading* BOREIN APELDOORN, *who carries a blanket.*)

JULIANA: There he is, Frau Apeldoorn. I told you. I told you. (*Running to* JAN) I came as fast as I could, Jan. She was in the barn when I got there, and I did not know it. Hasn't Vincent come back yet?

JAN: No, but it will be all right now. Thank you, Juliana.

GRANDFATHER: First, we have to find something to plug this leak, Jan, and then we will get your finger out.

BOREIN APELDOORN (*Going to* JAN): I have brought ointment for his finger and a blanket to wrap him in. The poor boy. All night in this April cold. He'll catch his death. (VINCENT *enters half-running, followed by* ADRIAN HAAS, *carrying a box.*)

VINCENT (*Yelling as he enters*): Jan! Jan, I'm back. I have the Bovenmeester with me. (*He sees the others.*) Oh! I have kept you waiting too long, but I ran as fast as I could.

JAN: It is all right, Vincent. It is all right. You came in time.

HAAS: I have brought mortar and stone to fix the leak. (*He joins the others at the leak.*) Easy now. Here, ease his finger out gently.

BOREIN APELDOORN: Men! (*Takes salve from her pocket*) Here, put this around his finger, and then it will slide out more easily.

HAAS: There, it's coming. There. It's out. (*Helps* JAN *away from the dike*) If you will take care of him, I'll fix this leak. Again a Dutchman has beaten the sea! (*He bends over and works on the dike.*)

GRANDFATHER (*Helping* JAN *a few feet from the leak, while* BOREIN APELDOORN *covers his shoulders with a blanket.*): Here, Jan, sit here for a moment, and Borein Apeldoorn will have that finger right in a minute.

BOREIN APELDOORN: You have the biggest finger in all Holland now, Jan.

GRANDFATHER: And the biggest heart!

HAAS: There, it's plugged now. (*Standing up and coming to* JAN) And how's our hero?

JAN: I'm no hero. I just put my finger in a hole, that's all.

HAAS: You did a good deal more than that. You saved Haarlem from the sea.

GRANDFATHER: Even more than that, Bovenmeester. Jan has proved again that a leak cannot show itself anywhere in Holland, but that a good stout Dutch finger will be there ready to stop it, at any cost. Somebody will one day build a statue for you, Jan, and on it he will write, "To honor the boy who symbolizes the eternal struggle of Holland against the sea."

BOREIN APELDOORN: You men, building monuments with your words! What our hero needs more than statues is his breakfast. I wish I had thought to bring something for him to eat. (NETTY *enters, running and carrying her basket.*)

NETTY: Jan! Jan, are you here?

JAN (*Starting to stand*): Over here, Netty.

NETTY (*Coming to him*): I came as soon as I could, Jan. And I brought you something. (*Reaches into her basket*) Breakfast. (*She brings out a covered jug and a piece of pastry.*) Milk and kuchen. (JAN *takes them and eats hungrily.*)

BOREIN APELDOORN: Now there's a Dutch woman for you. She knows enough to feed her hero.

VINCENT: Well, I say three cheers for Jan van Hoof, the hero of Haarlem.

JAN: And I say, have you got another piece of kuchen, Netty? (*All laugh as the curtain falls.*)

THE END

OUR SISTER, SITYA
(Indonesia)

Author's Notes on OUR SISTER, SITYA

The oldest of all drama on the island of Java, Indonesia, is the *wayang orang*, the "human puppet" theater, so called because all of its plays are adaptations of shadow and puppet plays. The stories for this traditional theater form come from the Indonesian versions of the great Hindu epics, the *Ramayana* and *Mahabharata*. The *wayang orang* is highly formalized drama—the characters are so familiar, and the make-up so conventional, that an Indonesian audience can tell from an actor's mere appearance who he is and what he will do in the play.

The story from which *Our Sister, Sitya* is adapted comes from the *Mahabharata*. It deals with the devotion of one person for another and the way in which this devotion brings about a happy ending.

Although this is "live" theater, there is one holdover from the puppet-theater—the puppet master. Known in Indonesian theater as the *dalang*, he no longer pulls the strings that make the actors move, but serves as a narrator who explains parts of the play.

Our Sister, Sitya

Characters

DALANG, *the narrator*
RAMA, *the prince*
SITYA, *his sister, the princess*
ARDJUNA, *their father, the king*
JITTITH, *their mother, the queen*
SEDYO, *the giant of blindness*
RAHAJOE, *the giant of force*
PAKU, *the King of Death*

TIME: *The distant past.*
SETTING: *The throne room of* ARDJUNA.
AT RISE: *The giant,* RAHAJOE, *is sitting on the throne.*
RAMA, *the prince, lies helpless on the floor, his head cushioned in* SITYA's *lap.* ARDJUNA *and* JITTITH, *the king and queen of the land, are downstage left. Sitting back of* ARDJUNA, *with his hands over the king's eyes so that he cannot see, is* SEDYO, *the giant of blindness.* DALANG *enters downstage right, bows to the audience and then speaks.*

DALANG: I am Dalang, the puppet master, and these are my puppets. Oh, don't look for any strings. They are

97

living puppets—a fact that almost puts me out of a job. But let me prove my usefulness for you. I will tell you what is happening. That young prince there (*Points to* RAMA) is dying, and his sister there (*Points to* SITYA) doesn't want to let him go. Her name is Sitya, and she loves her brother. Besides, things are in a terrible condition here in their kingdom. You see that great huge beast sitting on the king's throne? (*Points to* RAHAJOE) He doesn't belong there. He has seized the throne from the rightful king, Ardjuna. That's the poor old fellow over there. He is blind now, for the great beast, Sedyo, the giant of blindness, holds his eyes. That's the queen with him, Jittith, and she is very sad. They are all sad. Evil days have come upon them, and the future looks black. Death will surely come, and when he comes he'll take Rama with him. But do not fear. With a devotion like Sitya's, there is bound to be a way. All right, puppets, come alive. (*He claps his hands, and the characters start moving.*) My job is done; and now like a good puppet master, I must stay out of sight. (*Exits*)

RAMA: Has death come yet, my faithful sister?

SITYA: Hush, my brother. If Paku, the King of Death, should come, I shall ask him not to take you. And perhaps he will not come at all.

SEDYO: Ha, tell him the truth. He will come and drag you off, Rama. And then I shall blind your sister as I now blind your father.

ARDJUNA: Why do you persecute us? What have we ever done to you?

RAHAJOE: How silly good people are. Do you think evil bothers only people who have done evil? We much prefer to bother people who have never done us any harm.

SEDYO: We are not such fools as to bother people who harm us. It is much easier to blind you good fools.

ARDJUNA: But why have you worked your evil against *my* family?

RAHAJOE: Because you are good and we are evil, that's why.

SEDYO: Nothing could really be simpler, if you think about it.

SITYA: Do not talk to them, Father. Evil may come even to the good, but we do not have to listen to the voices of the brutes.

RAHAJOE: Ho. Ho. You will listen to us. You cannot get away from us.

RAMA: I wish that I were strong enough to drag you from that throne.

SEDYO: You, ho, ho! You, my young prince, will not have to listen to us long. Soon Paku will come with his golden noose and lead you off to his Kingdom of the Dead.

RAHAJOE: Then, what fun we shall have with your mother and with your sister.

SEDYO: Yes, with your sister, Sitya, especially. The saintly Sitya who comforts the sick and feeds the poor and deals kindly with the young and the old. Who will deal kindly with her now?

RAHAJOE: No one, for we shall make her dance on red hot coals.

SEDYO: And scrub the floor of the earth until she comes to water and until all the flesh is off her knuckles.

RAMA (*Trying to rise*): If I could just get on my feet, I'd . . .

SITYA: Hush, my brother, and rest. What we cannot stop, we must endure with patience. Do you remember when I broke my doll and cried? You came to me and told me that one does not cry over broken dolls and spilled milk, for tears do not help them, and only weaken us.

RAMA: Our sister, Sitya, has learned well from the sorrows of childhood, and her brother Rama learns from her wisdom. I am ready to go with Paku when he comes, but it is hard to leave when one is needed.

SITYA: Perhaps he will delay his visit.

JITTITH: I am an old woman, and I have seen Paku come many times. But he is kind. He comes as a friend.

ARDJUNA: And he is fair. Perhaps he will listen to you.

SEDYO: Perhaps! Ho. Ho. Perhaps, perhaps, perhaps. Paku will come and yank you off with his noose. Drag you off like a pig to the butcher.

RAHAJOE: Perhaps! Ho. Ho. Perhaps, he will bring medicine to cure Rama. Ho. Ho.

SEDYO: That would be a fine thing if the King of Death should bring the means to keep himself away. Ho. Ho. (PAKU *enters. He wears a white robe, and stands very straight.*)

PAKU: Quiet, you beasts that walk like men. (RAHAJOE *cowers on the throne, and* SEDYO *tries to hide behind* ARDJUNA.)

SITYA: You are Paku?

PAKU: I am he: Paku, King of Death.

SITYA: And you have come to take my brother?

PAKU (*Taking a gold braided rope, fixed like a noose, from under his robe*): I have. (*Pause*) Do not weep, and do not plead. I know your virtues, Sitya. I have watched your devotion. I know how you love your brother. I know your kindness to all the people you meet. Many now in *my* kingdom still speak of you with love. And though I admire you, yet I will not spare your brother. He must go with me.

SITYA: I would take his place. Please take me in his place.

PAKU: You are a brave girl, but no. I have vowed that all your pleading for your brother will not save him. And when I vow, I cannot be changed. It is my nature.

RAHAJOE: Ha. Ha. I told you that nothing you could say would save your brother.

SEDYO: Though Paku may hate us, yet he helps us make slaves of you.

PAKU: Quiet, you beasts. Or you shall find that although I would not have you in *my* kingdom, I am still not without power over you.

SITYA: But what will my father and mother do?

PAKU: How thoughtful you are. Even now you think of others. Truly, Sitya, I am sorry that I vowed not to be moved by your tears, for if I had not, I would leave Rama. I pity you, Sitya.

SITYA: Rather I would that you pity my father.

PAKU: I do. But I must take Rama with me now. (*He slips the noose over* RAMA's *head, so that it fits loosely around his throat.* RAMA *rises and stands ready to go with* PAKU.)

SITYA: How can you pity my father and leave him here, blind and without his throne?

PAKU: All right. I will grant you three wishes. That should show my pity.

SITYA: Any three wishes?

PAKU (*Smiles*): I know what you are thinking. Yes, I will grant you *any* three wishes, but—and note this—each wish must be for your father. You may wish nothing for yourself or for your brother. You understand?

SITYA: I am humbly pleased.

PAKU: Or if you prefer, I will give you all a girl could desire: riches, security, and fame . . . and blessed forgetfulness of this woe at home.

SITYA: The only way I could forget this woe at home would be to have this woe go away.

PAKU: Or you could forget father, mother, and brother.

SITYA: In happiness or in woe, I would never want to forget them.

PAKU: I knew as much. But hurry, for I must go. (*Takes a step, with* RAMA *following behind.*) Hurry, I haven't all day. What are your wishes? And remember, they can be only for your father. And only three.

SITYA: I wish . . . I wish first of all that my father could be freed from the beast that holds his eyes, so that he might see again.

PAKU: It shall be done. (*He points his finger at* SEDYO.) Depart, beast that blinds men's eyes.

SEDYO (*Releasing* ARDJUNA *and crawling back*): I go. I go. (*To* SITYA) But do not think that you have won so much, Princess. Your father now sees, but just remember this. . . .

ARDJUNA (*Standing*): I see. I see again. What a glorious thing is sight!

SEDYO: You see all right. Now think about this. The first sight that you see is the departure of your son forever. Is sight so wonderful, old king? Ha. Ha.

PAKU (*Shouting at* SEDYO): Depart from here and never

more return. Or I shall cast you deep into the sea where
fish shall nibble at your toes and seaweed choke you.
Go!

SEDYO (*Crawling off-stage left*): I go. I go, mighty Paku.
But all of you remember me. You may wish I still held
your eyes. (SEDYO *exits left.*)

PAKU: Your first wish has been granted, and I hope you
are the happier for it. (*Takes a step to the right with*
RAMA) When one asks favors of Paku, he should be
sure that he knows what he wants. With Paku, everything is final. (*He starts to take another step.*)

SITYA: But you promised me three wishes.

PAKU: I promised three and I shall give three—if you ask
nothing for yourself or for Rama, your brother. But
hurry.

SITYA: For my second wish, I ask that you restore my
father's throne to him.

PAKU: It is a good wish, one that I am glad to grant.
Surely it is bad for all when the rightful man is out
of power and evil sits on the throne. (*Points his finger
at* RAHAJOE) Depart, rude force, and tell the story of
what happens when power alone tries to rule over men.
Tell of your downfall and be a lesson to all your evil
brothers. Leave the throne of Ardjuna at once.

RAHAJOE (*Stumbles from the throne and almost falls*):
I knew this would come, and I am ready for it. But
are you pleased now, old king?

ARDJUNA: No man who should rule is pleased to rule. But
I am happy that there is a power of goodness before
which evil itself must stand in fear. And I shall try to
rule always with the knowledge that a king rules only
to serve.

PAKU: Take your throne, Ardjuna. Your merit deserves it. (ARDJUNA *and* JITTITH, *arm in arm, march slowly toward the throne.*) It is well that your queen go with you. Again, Sitya, you have chosen well and in proper order. First a man must see, so that he may know his duty. Then he must be free to do his duty. You are a wise and good daughter, and I would that I might bring you personal happiness. But . . . (*Takes another step with* RAMA)

SITYA: But King Paku, wait. Please wait.

PAKU: I know the wish that is in your heart, and I cannot grant it. I cannot leave your brother.

RAHAJOE (*Who stumbles to stage left as* ARDJUNA *and* JITTITH *walk toward the throne*): Ardjuna, you now rule again. But think of this. After you, what comes? You now have no son to succeed you. Your days of rule are numbered, and what comes next, no one knows. I will be back on that throne soon. I always return to an empty throne.

PAKU: Get from my sight, you hyena.

RAHAJOE (*Runs over, cringing*): With no son to succeed you, you'll remember me, Ardjuna. (*To* PAKU) I go. I go. I know my weakness. I am no fool. (*He exits left.*)

PAKU: He is gone. And I must go, too. (*Starts off right with* RAMA, *then pauses as* ARDJUNA *speaks.*)

ARDJUNA: Yes, he's gone. But I will remember him. A kingdom that cannot see its future is already living in the past. What will come when I leave with you? What will then come to this land of Java?

PAKU: That you will have to wait and see. But I must leave.

SITYA: Wait. My third wish! I still have my third wish.

PAKU: All right. Make your third wish, so long as it is for your father and not for your brother or yourself. But hurry.

SITYA: I am grateful, King Paku, that you have chased away the beast that blinded my father.

PAKU: Yes, yes. But hurry. You are a brave girl that keeps Paku in conversation. Do not be too bold.

SITYA: I shall be as brief as I can. And I am grateful that you have returned my father's throne to him, not only for my father's sake but for all those who live on this island of Java, and who have suffered under the cruel rule of Rahajoe.

PAKU: Yes, yes. But make your wish. Is there nothing more your father needs?

SITYA: Just this, King Paku. He needs his son. Give my father his son as you have so graciously given him back his sight and kingdom.

PAKU: I said it! And well you know it. I said I would not give you back your brother.

SITYA: I ask not as a sister for her brother's life, but as a daughter for her father's happiness. Give me not back Rama for my brother, nor even for his own sake. But give my father back his son so that the order of the kingdom may continue.

PAKU: You are brave and kind, Sitya. This I knew. But you are also clever, and you have bested me. (*Removes noose from* RAMA's *throat*) I shall keep my promise and give you your third wish. Your father's son is restored to him. (RAMA *now comes to life and looks about.*)

RAMA: Father! Father, I am well.

ARDJUNA (*Going to* RAMA): My son, you are restored to me.

PAKU: I give Rama an extension—one lifetime. Live wisely, young Prince, and do the things that become the son of a king . . . and (*Smiles*) the brother of Sitya. (*To* SITYA) Goodbye, little princess. Even the King of Death must acknowledge your powers. There is a strength in goodness, kindness, and devotion that makes even Death glad to leave empty-handed. Do not remember *me*, but remember this. (*He exits off-stage right, as the whole family moves to stage center. Curtain.*)

THE END

THE COURTERS
(Italy)

Author's Notes on THE COURTERS

"The Courters" is based on the *Commedia dell' Arte,* an Italian comedy form that flourished in the sixteenth century. The theater in which such comedies were performed was much like a modern circus. The actors of the *Commedia dell' Arte,* like modern circus clowns, were trained to hold the attention of an active, fun-loving crowd.

These actors were what we would call character types: the *Capitano,* the bragging soldier; *Pantalone,* the foolish old man; *Flavio* and *Isabella,* the young lovers; *Arlecchino* and *Brighella,* the rascally servants or *zannis,* as they were called. Except for the lovers, all of the actors were made up and dressed to get as many laughs as possible. The *Commedia dell' Arte* is the art of acting out what people do and is not an imitation of people themselves. The actor playing *Pantalone,* for example, is not playing a foolish *man;* rather, he is playing the *foolishness* in man. The *Commedia dell' Arte* doesn't make fun of people. It makes fun of the things that people do and say.

Although the plots of the plays were used over and over again, and the same characters were used in many plays, the actors made up new lines for each performance, told new jokes, performed new pranks. And they improvised while they were performing. The actors knew their character types, knew what they would say in any given situation.

The plays of the *Commedia dell' Arte* were not written down as are modern plays so we have no actual copy of one; but we know the plots and the characters used in them and even some of the lines spoken by these characters. The plot used for "The Courters" and the characters who appear in the play are the same as those the people of Italy saw in 1550.

The Courters

Characters

ARLECCHINO, *the foolish servant*
BRIGHELLA, *the crafty servant*
PANTALONE, *a foolish old bachelor, uncle of Flavio.*
DOTTORE, *a learned doctor of Bologna and a friend of Pantalone; a foolish old man and the guardian of Isabella.*
FLAVIO, *a handsome young man, in love with Isabella.*
ISABELLA, *a beautiful young lady, in love with Flavio.*

SETTING: *A city square in one of the towns of Italy in the sixteenth century.*

AT RISE: BRIGHELLA *walks on stage from left, and* ARLECCHINO, *rushing in from the right, runs into him and falls down.* BRIGHELLA *stands and looks down at* ARLECCHINO, *obviously much disgusted.*

BRIGHELLA: Well, Foolish One, why don't you look where you're going?
ARLECCHINO: I couldn't. I was racing him, and I had to see where he was going.
BRIGHELLA: Racing whom? I don't see anyone.
ARLECCHINO: I'm sitting on him. (*He bends over so that*

109

he is standing on his feet and hands facing the ground.)
See?

BRIGHELLA: I see nothing, stupid, except you and your own shadow.

ARLECCHINO: That's him. My shadow. I was racing him.

BRIGHELLA: You were racing your own shadow?

ARLECCHINO: I wasn't really racing him. (*In a stage whisper*) I just said that to fool him. I was really trying to lose him. He's always following me around. Spying on me, I'll bet.

BRIGHELLA: Spying on your great empty brain, you zany. Running away from your own shadow and running into people in the street. What a fool you are!

ARLECCHINO: It's just as well I ran into *you*. Flavio, my master, sent me to find you.

BRIGHELLA: And I'm looking for him. Where is he?

ARLECCHINO: I don't know where *he* is. He told me to find *you*.

BRIGHELLA: What were you supposed to tell me when you found me?

ARLECCHINO: I wasn't supposed to tell you anything. It is my master who wants to speak to you.

BRIGHELLA: Blockhead! Where is your master?

ARLECCHINO: Why should I find him for you? You're not my master.

BRIGHELLA (*Aside to audience*): The rogue has some sense in his nonsense, but fortunately I don't have to find it. Here comes Flavio now. (*Enter* FLAVIO *from right.*)

FLAVIO: Ah, Brighella, there you are. Didn't Arlecchino tell you I was looking for you?

BRIGHELLA: He did, but he didn't tell me where I could find you.

FLAVIO (*To* ARLECCHINO): Why not, you blockhead?

ARLECCHINO: You told me to find him. You didn't tell me to find you.

FLAVIO: Stop! Stop! You're making my head ache. (*To* BRIGHELLA) I need your sharp wits, my friend.

BRIGHELLA: Because we are such great friends, they are yours . . . if you pay me, of course.

FLAVIO: Gladly, my friend, if you can save my romance. Pantalone wants to marry.

BRIGHELLA: Your uncle?

FLAVIO: The same. And if he marries, I shall not receive a penny of my inheritance.

BRIGHELLA: This is serious business. Whom does the old man want to marry?

FLAVIO: That's the silliest part of it. He is not interested in anyone. He just wants to marry.

ARLECCHINO: But she must be willing to marry him. That he insists on.

FLAVIO: Be quiet, blockhead.

ARLECCHINO: He told me himself. He will marry no woman who will not marry him. It would be too ridiculous, he said.

FLAVIO: If you don't be quiet, I shall beat your head until it is as scrambled as an omelet.

BRIGHELLA: Wait a minute. A plot begins to brew.

FLAVIO: A good plot?

BRIGHELLA: A bad one for your uncle's plans to marry.

FLAVIO: Good, it will be double mercy. It will save both him and the woman foolish enough to marry him.

BRIGHELLA: Arlecchino, run and fetch Pantalone here.

ARLECCHINO: You are not my master.

FLAVIO: Do as you are told, you rascal.

ARLECCHINO (*Mumbling as he moves off left*): Last week when Brighella told me to steal food from the pantry for a party for us servants, Flavio beat me for doing what Brighella told me. Now he orders me about. What's a poor, honest servant to do?

FLAVIO: Run, you rascal. (ARLECCHINO *leaps in the air as though he had been shot and then runs off.*) Now, my friend, what is your plan?

BRIGHELLA: Your old uncle doesn't like to appear foolish.

FLAVIO: True, and he wouldn't need to appear foolish if he were not such a foolish old man. Do you remember last year when he wanted to invest all our money in an expedition to the moon to look for green cheese?

BRIGHELLA: And the year before when he wanted to cross an oyster with a cabbage to raise pearls as big as cabbages.

FLAVIO: And he would have done it, too, if you had not told him how foolish he would appear if he succeeded only in raising cabbages as small as pearls.

BRIGHELLA: Good then. Now, what is the one thing he fears in marriage?

FLAVIO: Having been a bachelor these sixty years or more, he fears nothing. And he will have any woman who will marry him.

BRIGHELLA: But suppose he found that his marriage plans would simply make a fool of him?

FLAVIO: They will, but I don't see how you will convince him of the fact.

BRIGHELLA: Very simple. Suppose he courted someone and it turned out to be a monstrous joke. Don't you think that would make the old boy more satisfied with the life of a bachelor?

FLAVIO: That's really the only life he wants. He told me he hated women, all of them, but that maybe he would like marriage.

BRIGHELLA: I think I can make him hate marriage as well if he sees that to love marriage and hate women is a foolish thing.

FLAVIO: You are indeed a great rascal. That might be the one thing that would keep him from the altar. But when he discovers he has been duped, he may disinherit me and I won't be able to marry anyway.

BRIGHELLA: But he won't be duped. I will make him think that he has exposed another.

FLAVIO: If you can do that. . . .

BRIGHELLA: Quick. Hide nearby. I would see him alone.

FLAVIO: I'll go. (*Disappears off stage left as* ARLECCHINO *and* PANTALONE *come on right*)

PANTALONE (*Puffing and panting*): Well, here we are. Now, tell me what it is you want.

ARLECCHINO: Brighella, he wishes to speak to you.

PANTALONE: You fool, you made me run all the way here to tell me this?

ARLECCHINO: Someone was listening where I found you, and we had to run away from him.

PANTALONE: I saw no one.

ARLECCHINO (*In a loud stage whisper*): My shadow.

PANTALONE: Your shadow! What do I care what your shadow hears?

ARLECCHINO: I saw your shadow, too.

PANTALONE: My shadow? Well, that is a different matter. I do not trust that fellow. He is always peering over my shoulder whenever I think I'm alone. (*To* BRIGHELLA) Well, what is it you want of me, fellow?

BRIGHELLA: I hear that you would marry.

PANTALONE: Well, what if I would? I won't marry you.

BRIGHELLA: Would you marry someone with a great fortune?

PANTALONE: Only if she will have me. I'll marry no woman who will not marry me.

BRIGHELLA: Oh, she'll marry you, and what a woman she is! Tall like a palm tree! She is a woman who knows how to make her husband happy. She hates to spend money on herself and loves to spend it on her husband.

PANTALONE (*Reaching above his head*): Tall like a palm tree?

BRIGHELLA: Even taller.

PANTALONE: And loves to spend money on her husband?

BRIGHELLA: Just so.

PANTALONE: Then she's the woman for me. I'll marry her.

BRIGHELLA: First, you must win her.

PANTALONE: I knew there was a catch—with all her money.

BRIGHELLA: I shall help you.

PANTALONE: I put myself in your hands if you put me in her arms.

BRIGHELLA: Then listen to my plan. She will be here shortly. Go home and dress like a woman. Then come back, and I'll introduce you.

PANTALONE: Dress like a woman? What for? I don't want to do anything silly.

BRIGHELLA: If you want to marry her, you'll listen to me. She wants to marry, but she is very much afraid that she will marry the wrong man. But if a woman were to tell her what a great catch you are, what a wonderful man you are. . . .

PANTALONE: Who will tell her what a wonderful man I am?

BRIGHELLA: Why, you will, of course.

PANTALONE: If anyone is to tell her I am wonderful, I will have to do it. But will she believe me?

BRIGHELLA: I am sure she will.

PANTALONE: Then I'm not at all sure I want to marry her. A woman foolish enough to believe that would make a foolish wife.

BRIGHELLA: But she will believe you because she will not know that you are the man, Pantalone. In your disguise, she will think that you are Madam Pantanella.

PANTALONE: Madam Pantanella. That's good.

BRIGHELLA: And it will be Madam Pantanella who will tell her what a wonderful man Pantalone is. And then when she says, "That is the man I must marry," you take off the disguise and say, "I am the man."

PANTALONE: When she says *marry*, I take off my wig and say, "I am the man." Good. Good. Very good. Well, I'm off. (*Exit* PANTALONE *running*)

ARLECCHINO: He's in for trouble. His shadow was with him all the time and listening. And it ran after him. (*Enter* ISABELLA)

ISABELLA: Alas, alack! The day is black, and I think my heart will surely break in half. Alas, alack!

BRIGHELLA: Now, what is the matter, Lady Isabella?

ISABELLA: My guardian has told me he will marry. And if he marries, then Flavio and I can never wed, for I'll have no dowry.

BRIGHELLA: Old Dottore, too! This must be the season for old fools to shed their grey hairs and creep backward in time like a crab.

ISABELLA: But perhaps no one will have him. Perhaps.

BRIGHELLA: Who's the lady?

ISABELLA: There's no particular lady. Dottore will marry any woman as long as she's willing. Alas and alack. If there were some lady he loved, I would give him my blessings. Alas. Alack.

BRIGHELLA: Just like Pantalone. But in this double folly may be double fortune. I shall use one fool to bait the trap for the other.

ISABELLA: I don't understand. Alas. Alack. But if you don't do something, Flavio and I are lost. Alas. Alack.

BRIGHELLA: I shall do something, but I'll let Flavio explain our plan to you. He's over there. (*Points off stage*) And hurry. Here comes your ancient guardian now, and I want to see him alone.

ISABELLA: Flavio here! Oh, joy and happiness. (*Exit* ISABELLA *running*)

ARLECCHINO: Since this seems to be the season for fools and love, I might marry too.

BRIGHELLA: You? And what would you do with your shadow?

ARLECCHINO: He can do what I do. Find a wife of his own. (*Enter* DOTTORE, *his face buried in a large book.* ARLECCHINO *runs in front him and bends over.* DOTTORE *tumbles over him and picks himself up, reading his book all the while without realizing what has happened.*)

BRIGHELLA (*Shouting at him*): Dottore! Dottore! (*As*

DOTTORE *doesn't notice him, he raps on his head as though he were knocking on a door.*) Open the door. Open the door.

DOTTORE: Come in. Come in.

BRIGHELLA: I can't. The door is locked.

DOTTORE: I'll come down and let you in. (*He looks up from his book, for the first time aware of his surroundings.*) Well, bless my books. Where am I?

BRIGHELLA: You were consulting me about the woman you will marry.

DOTTORE: Was I? Oh, yes. Of course. Of course.

BRIGHELLA: You *are* resolved to marry?

DOTTORE: The stars are resolved. Last night when I read the heavens, Venus twinkled at me and whispered, "The time is ripe."

ARLECCHINO: And the groom is a little over-ripe.

DOTTORE: But, where is my bride?

BRIGHELLA: You haven't met her yet.

DOTTORE: Haven't met her. I must make a note of that. (*He writes in the book, speaking as he writes.*) Meet bride.

BRIGHELLA: Of course, it is all arranged. You will wed the fabulous, glorious, beautified Madam Pantanella.

DOTTORE (*Writing in book*): The fabulous, glorious, beautified Madam Pantanella.

BRIGHELLA: But, of course, first you must win her.

DOTTORE (*Writes in book*): Win her. (*Looking up with surprise*) And how will I do that? The stars said nothing about winning.

BRIGHELLA: Go home and dress like a woman. When you return, she will be here, and I will introduce you. Then you will tell her what a wonderful fellow Dottore **is,** and when she says, "Oh I must marry him," you will tear off your wig and say, "I am the man."

DOTTORE: I like telling her what a wonderful man I am, but why must I dress like a woman?

BRIGHELLA: Would you believe a man who told you he was wonderful?

DOTTORE: Not just any man. But *I* am wonderful.

BRIGHELLA: True, but you will be able to expound on your virtues so much better when you can speak through another's lips.

DOTTORE: True, I am modest. I really am much better than I think myself to be. I tell myself that all the time.

BRIGHELLA: Then go prepare. Arlecchino will help you.

ARLECCHINO: He goes home a groom, and he'll come back a bride.

BRIGHELLA: Madam Pantanella will be here waiting for you, Madam Dolores.

DOTTORE: Madam Dolores! Oh, what a beautiful name that is. It's the most beautiful name I ever heard. I think I shall marry Madam Dolores.

BRIGHELLA: But *you* are Madam Dolores.

DOTTORE: Then it's out of the question. One can't marry himself, not even a fine fellow like me. (*Exit* DOTTORE *and* ARLECCHINO.)

BRIGHELLA (*To audience*): This is surely the season of fools when old men who thought themselves too wise to marry in youth stagger to folly in age. But it has been ever thus. The world is full of foolish folk who want to be wise without learning, good without trying, and happy without laughing. And you young fellows out there (*Points to audience*), learn what you will be now, for when the years pile on, you'll be too busy defending your faults ever to get rid of them. (*Looks up at the sky through his fingers as though telling time*) But by this time, our courters are ready. So enough of the philosophy and on with the play. Here comes Pantalone now, dressed for folly. (*Enter* PANTALONE *dressed as a woman*.) Ah, Madam Pantanella, you would charm the Sphinx, solid stone that it is. You look wonderful.

PANTALONE: Indeed I do. When I saw myself in the mirror, I almost proposed. And do you know, I was afraid that I would look the fool in this garb.

BRIGHELLA (*To audience*): These amorous old fools are only in love with their own foolishness. But, here comes Dottore now. (*To* PANTALONE) Ah, here comes your bride-to-be, Madam Dolores.

PANTALONE: Madam Dolores. That's not a very pretty name. I do so wish that I weren't I so that I could marry me. (*Enter* DOTTORE *dressed as a woman, with* ARLECCHINO)

BRIGHELLA: Hush! Here comes the blushing bride now.

PANTALONE: She's certainly a big one.

BRIGHELLA: I'll introduce you in a few minutes, and you know what to say, don't you?

PANTALONE: I have it by heart. When she says, "That's the man I want to marry," I pull off this wig and say, "I am the man." But I do wish Madam Pantanella were the woman.

BRIGHELLA: Forget yourself or you'll never win the lady. Now, wait here, and I shall bring her to you. (BRI-

GHELLA *goes to* DOTTORE, *and* PANTALONE *moves up-stage away from them.*) Ah, Madam Dolores, you look wonderful.

DOTTORE: Indeed, I do. And what a wonderful name I have . . . Madam Dolores. Like bells ringing.

ARLECCHINO: Indeed it is like . . . like cow bells.

BRIGHELLA: Madam Dolores is a very fine name, but don't forget it is Madam Pantanella you are courting.

DOTTORE: Madam Pantanella! That's not a very pretty name. Maybe she would be willing to change it to Madam Dolores. Oh, that's such a pretty name.

BRIGHELLA: If you remember what you are supposed to say, you may even change it to Madam Dottore.

DOTTORE: Oh, I know it by heart. When she says, "That's the man I want to marry," I pull off my wig and say, "I am the man." But I do wish her name were Madam Dolores.

BRIGHELLA: Good, then come along with me now, and I'll introduce you. (BRIGHELLA *takes* DOTTORE's *arm and leads him to* PANTALONE. *The introductions are carried on upstage in dumb show, while the spoken action continues downstage.*)

ARLECCHINO (*To audience*): I am, you should know by now, a very stupid fellow. And indeed when I talk to a smart fellow like Brighella, sometimes I even know that I am stupid. But what is the sense of good sense in this world? Pantalone is a wise man in business and Dottore is a very learned scholar, but they are fools for all of that. In this world, the foolish are wise, for the wise want to be foolish. (FLAVIO *and* ISABELLA *enter from stage left and join* ARLECCHINO. *They tip-toe, looking carefully at the courters.*)

FLAVIO: Arlecchino, how goes the plot? Is the courting season almost over for our guardians?

ARLECCHINO: It is almost the moment. Soon you should be able to hear the cuckoo sing.

ISABELLA: My guardian makes a better woman than he ever made a man. He looks better with his head out of a book, even a head like his. (BRIGHELLA *comes down, leaving the two old men gesturing foolishly in dumb show as each tries to tell the other what a fine man he is. They are obviously not listening to each other.*)

BRIGHELLA: If they would ever listen to each other, our whole plot would be exposed. But they are both speaking so fondly of themselves that neither can hear the other. But do not worry, young lovers, you are as safe as an old man's vanity, which is an old proverb meaning you are as safe as the stars. (*The* SERVANTS *and the lovers now speak in dumb show, and the two old men can be heard.*)

PANTALONE: In brief, Madam Dolores, Senor Pantalone is the wisest, the best, the handsomest, the kindest, the youngest old man that ever sniffed the air of Italy.

DOTTORE: And Madam Pantanella, it therefore follows that if you are seeking a husband, you can do no better than the magnificent Dottore, the wisest, most learned man, the greatest mind in all Italy. Truly a fine man.

PANTALONE ⎫
            ⎬ (*Together*): He is the man you must marry.
DOTTORE   ⎭

(*Pause*) Marry? (*Each reaches up, pulls off his own wig, and bows.*) So, Madam, I am the man.

PANTALONE: Dottore! What are you doing here?

DOTTORE: Someone knocked at my door. Was it you?

PANTALONE: You are trying to trick me. To make a fool of me.

DOTTORE: You are trying to make a fool of me. That's what I get for letting you talk me into marrying.

PANTALONE: I talk you into marrying? I would think an old fool like you would have better sense.

DOTTORE: Old fool, am I? I thought you were my friend.

PANTALONE: I thought you were *my* friend. My nephew, Flavio, was to marry your ward, Isabella.

DOTTORE: Ah, ha, liar! It was my ward, Isabella, that was to marry your nephew, Flavio. (*They argue in dumb show while downstage action becomes audible again.*)

ISABELLA: Oh, dear, oh dear! We may have cured them of our marrying as well as their own. Now they are fighting.

FLAVIO: And threatening to break our engagement.

ISABELLA: Alas.

FLAVIO: Alack.

BRIGHELLA: Have no fears. I will save the day. (*Calls upstage to them and then starts toward them*) Gentlemen, gentlemen, are you ready?

PANTALONE: I am ready all right, ready to fight a duel.

DOTTORE: Name your weapon, you sweetheart stealer. Oh, when shall I ever see my fair Dolores again?

PANTALONE: Weapon, sir? Are you threatening me with with a weapon?

DOTTORE: Threatening? Indeed, yes. You betrayed me.

BRIGHELLA (*Now with them*): Gentlemen, gentlemen, have you forgotten why we are here? There is to be a wedding.

PANTALONE: Not for me. I shall never marry. And I

wouldn't marry Madam Dolores if she were as rich as old King Midas.

DOTTORE: Nor will I ever marry. And I wouldn't marry Madam Pantanella if every star in the heavens spelled her name.

BRIGHELLA: But, gentlemen, it is not *your* wedding day. This was the day Flavio and Isabella were to marry. Have you forgotten?

DOTTORE: Forgotten? Indeed, I have not—now that you remind me.

PANTALONE: Flavio and Isabella! Of course. Better their wedding than my funeral.

DOTTORE: I was sure someone had knocked on my door. It must have been to call me to the wedding. (*To* PANTALONE) Are you the mother of the groom?

PANTALONE (*Aside to audience*): If I say I am, he will forget all this talk of weapons. (*Slapping the wig back on his head*) Are you the guardian of the bride?

DOTTORE: I am, madam.

PANTALONE: Then I shall take your arm, and you shall lead me to the church. (*They start off right, arm in arm. The lovers follow, arm and arm, and the servants following the lovers imitate them.*)

BRIGHELLA (*To audience*): Well, all's well that ends well, but I swear this was the silliest courtship that ever was. (*Curtain*)

THE END

BOSHIBARI AND THE TWO THIEVES
(Japan)

This play is a free adaptation of a Japanese Kyōgen farce, *Boshibari*. Although the Kyōgen farce, on first appearance, seems much like American slapstick comedy, it is basically a far different art. As it is now presented in Japan, the Kyōgen farce is a companion piece to the serious, formal Noh drama, Japan's most treasured classic art.

The Noh play has a history that goes back seven hundred years. Every dance step, every movement of the hand, every sound of the drum and flute, and every word in a Noh play has a conventional formal meaning. When an actor lifts his hands softly to his eyes, for example, it means grief; when he takes a step backward, it means surprise. The actors talk not only with words, but with sounds and movements.

The Kyōgen play, although a farce, belongs to this highly stylized art world; and an American children's production should stress formality.

This play deals with two servants who trick their master, a familiar situation in English literature of this age as well as in Japanese literature. Even the interest of the servants in performing with the quarterstaff, or jousting pole, is understandable to those who remember English history of about the same period.

Like the English of the age of Robin Hood, the Japanese were masters of the quarterstaff, a stout pole used in fighting. The quarterstaff, or jousting pole, was used as a weapon to knock a man down and hit him on the head; but for both the Japanese and the English, fighting with poles was an art as well. In the demonstrations which Taro and Jiro give in this play, they use formal movements with the quarterstaff, and when they bow, their hands are behind them holding the pole, thus making it easy for Daimyo to tie them to their own quarterstaffs.

Like American and English farce, the Kyōgen farce has about the same "lesson": Men are made fools of when they become vain. The servants are tied to their own poles when they become too proud of their accomplishment as jousters; and Daimyo is robbed of his apples when he becomes too certain that he has been successful.

Boshibari and the Two Thieves

Characters

TARO KAJA (*the Shite or principal actor*), *a servant*
DAIMYO (*the Ado or secondary actor*), *the master*
JIRO KAJA (*the Ko-ado or character actor*), *another servant*

SCENE 1

TIME: *Morning.*
SETTING: *The house of Daimyo.*
AT RISE: DAIMYO *walks on stage and bows formally to the audience.*

DAIMYO: I am Daimyo, a gentleman of Japan, and the master of this house. I have been told that two of my servants have been stealing into my apple orchard every time I go out on business. They have been eating the best of my fruit. This displeases me. Today business takes me away from home, and I must think of a way to match their cunning, a way to stop their stealing. (*Calls off-stage*) Jiro! Jiro, come here! (*To audience*) Jiro Kaja is one of the two rascals who has been stealing my apples. (JIRO *enters, carrying a quarterstaff, and bows to the audience.*) Jiro Kaja, I am not pleased. I am

127

not pleased at all. I am not pleased because I have received word that Taro Kaja has been misbehaving.

JIRO: Taro Kaja, my lord?

DAIMYO: Yes, Taro Kaja. He has been misbehaving during my absence, and I must find a way to stop him.

JIRO: I do not think it can be so, my lord.

DAIMYO: It is so. Now Taro is very clever and has proved skillful in getting out of tight places in the past. How can I be sure of catching him? Will you help me think of a way?

JIRO: My lord, I am sure that you are mistaken. Taro is as honest as the day is long.

DAIMYO: Then winter must be coming, for the days should be getting shorter and shorter.

JIRO: I am sure you have been misinformed, my lord. I am sure that he is not stealing apples from your orchard.

DAIMYO: Who said anything about stealing apples?

JIRO: Why, you did, my lord.

DAIMYO: I said nothing about stealing apples.

JIRO (*Putting his hand to his mouth as he speaks, to indicate that this is an aside to the audience and cannot be heard by* DAIMYO): I almost trapped myself that time. (*To* DAIMYO) It is hard to think ill of honest Taro, my lord, but if you need my help, of course, I shall give it.

DAIMYO: Good. What do you suggest?

JIRO: For what, my lord?

DAIMYO: To stop Taro from stealing my apples during my absence. What else have we been talking about?

JIRO: You said that you had said nothing about apples, my lord.

DAIMYO: I am now. Well, what do you suggest?

JIRO: I shall have to think on this. Let me see. Ah, yes.

(*He holds his quarterstaff up, like a cavalry officer presenting arms with his sword.*) Taro Kaja prides himself on his skill with the quarterstaff.

DAIMYO: I smell a plot brewing. Continue.

JIRO (*Demonstrating with his staff as he explains*): As you know, my lord, in the contest of the jousting pole, as it is practiced at the Royal Tournament, after a man has given his exhibition, he holds the pole above his head, thus (*Holds pole horizontally above head*), and bows, thus. (*Bows with pole held behind him.*)

DAIMYO: Yes, yes. What of it?

JIRO: It might be well, my lord, to ask Taro to give a short exhibition of his skill with the quarterstaff. When he is finished and is bowing, you need simply slip these ropes (*Draws four short ropes, which are tied in loops, from inside his blouse*) around Taro's hands and tie him to his own pole. It is a saying, my lord, that a thief without hands is on his way to being an honest man.

DAIMYO: Very good, Jiro. Very good. With his hands tied, Taro will not be able to steal my apples. You will receive your deserts for this, Jiro.

JIRO: This humble servant is rewarded with your approval, my lord. (*Bows*)

DAIMYO (*Calling off*): Taro. Taro Kaja, come here. (TARO *enters, carrying a quarterstaff. He bows to the audience.*) Taro, your loyal friend, Jiro, has been singing of your skill with the pole.

TARO: I am pleased, my lord, that my loyal friend, Jiro, speaks well of my poor talent.

DAIMYO: I am much impressed. I would see an exhibition, Taro.

TARO: My lord favors me too much.

DAIMYO: You may proceed. (TARO *gives a short exhibition with the quarterstaff, ending with the bow. As he bows,* DAIMYO *slips the ropes along the ends of the pole, thus binding* TARO's *wrists.*) Your lord is pleased, Taro, with your performance. I have never seen you better.

TARO: I am humble, my lord, in the warm sunshine of your words. But why have you bound my hands?

DAIMYO: Your lord is pleased with your performance with the quarterstaff, you rascal! But I am displeased that you have been performing in my apple orchard. Need I say more?

TARO: It is a foolish man, my lord, who will not learn from the roar of the lion.

DAIMYO: You are wise, Taro.

TARO: I am humble, my lord, before your praise.

DAIMYO (*Turning to* JIRO): Tell me, Jiro, was this not a fine exhibition?

JIRO: It was well done, my lord. You know my meaning.

TARO: My loyal friend, Jiro, is too kind.

JIRO: And my friend Taro is a fool. Posing and prancing before the lord as though you were the greatest pole jouster in Japan. (*He mocks* TARO's *performance with a final bow. As he does,* DAIMYO *ties his hands to the pole in the same manner as before.*) My lord, why have you tied my hands?

DAIMYO: Because you are as big a fool as Taro. Did you not know that I knew that you, too, were stealing my apples?

JIRO: The wisdom of my lord is like the brightness of the moon. It dispels even the shadows of night.

DAIMYO: Now I am safe to leave this house and go about

my business. And you two will remain tied until my return. This is a just punishment for stealing my apples every time I leave the house in your care. (DAIMYO *bows to audience and exits.*)

JIRO: This is a fine mess you got me into.

TARO: If you had not mocked me, he would not have caught you.

JIRO: If you had not been so foolish, I would not have mocked you.

TARO: If you had not betrayed me, I would not have been so foolish.

JIRO: Well, what are we to do?

TARO: Let us go to the orchard. I am so hungry for a juicy apple.

JIRO: What good will it do us to go to the fruit if we cannot eat it?

TARO: We could still reach the apples even with our hands tied.

JIRO: But we could not reach our mouths with the apple in our hand, and so we would only be beaten for our pains with nothing for our stomachs.

TARO: At least, we can go and smell the apples.

JIRO: We can at least do that. (*They bow to the audience and exit.*)

* * *

SCENE 2

TIME: *Later that morning.*

SETTING: *The orchard of Daimyo.*

AT RISE: DAIMYO *enters, bows to the audience, picks up the sign, "The House of Daimyo," bows again and exits. He returns with tree to which apples are tied. He also carries a sign reading, "The Orchard of Daimyo." After placing tree and sign in position he turns to audience and bows.*

DAIMYO: This is the garden of Daimyo, and (*Points*) this is one of the fine apple trees that grow in the garden. At this moment I am on my way to the city on business. (*Bows to audience and exits. Enter* JIRO *and* TARO *tied to their poles.*)

JIRO (*Going to the tree and sniffing the apples*): They smell delicious.

TARO: I am so hungry.

JIRO (*Picking one of the apples*): It is really quite simple to pick the fruit.

TARO (*With the same action*): Quite simple.

JIRO (*Holding it toward his mouth*): But it's impossible to get the fruit in my hand between my teeth.

TARO (*Trying without success*): Quite impossible.

JIRO: All of which is most depressing.

TARO: Quite depressing.

JIRO: Having the fruit in my hands makes me hungry.

TARO: Quite hungry.

JIRO: There must be a way.

TARO: Any way.

JIRO: There should be a way.

TARO: There *is* a way!

JIRO: What way?

TARO: Like this. (*He kneels before* JIRO *and holds up his fruit for* JIRO *to eat.*) If the lion and the mouse can serve one another, we should be able to do the same. You feed me, and I shall feed you.

JIRO: Indeed, this is the way.

TARO: Well, then, eat away. (*Enter* DAIMYO *who speaks to the audience while* JIRO *and* TARO *take turns feed-*

*ing each other. Each takes only a single bite and then
positions change.)*

DAIMYO: At this moment, while I am on my way to the
city, a thought comes to me. It is true that I have tied
the rascals' hands so they cannot feed themselves, but
they can feed one another. And knowing them, I know
the thought has also come into their minds. So I will
turn about and run back to the orchard, and the next
time you see me, I'll be entering this orchard. *(Bows
to audience and exits)*

JIRO: We have eaten two dozen of these apples.

TARO: Let's make it two dozen and one.

JIRO: It is odd, but the more I eat, the hungrier I am.

TARO: If we hurry, we can pick the orchard clean before
the master returns.

JIRO: It will serve him right for not trusting us. *(DAIMYO
enters, but they do not notice him.)*

DAIMYO *(To audience)*: You see, I was right. The rascals
have outwitted me. There they sit now, so deep in
apple cores they do not even observe my return. Oh,
I am so angry. *(Stamps foot. JIRO and TARO jump
around.)*

JIRO: The master has returned.

TARO: He has indeed.

JIRO: And it's time for us to go.

TARO: It is indeed. *(They bow formally to the audience
and run out.)*

DAIMYO *(To audience)*: It was ever thus. If you catch
two thieves, tie them apart, not together. *(He bows to
audience and then runs after them, shouting, "Thief!
Thief!" The curtain falls.)*

THE END

LICHA'S BIRTHDAY SERENADE
(*Mexico*)

Author's Notes on LICHA'S BIRTHDAY SERENADE

Mexico, our closest South-of-the-Border neighbor, is for many of us in the United States a vacation land, a land of dancing and singing, of bullfights and colorful costumes, of splendid cities like Mexico City and quaint little villages like San Marcos, hardly more than a cluster of adobe houses, that seem to belong to an earlier time. This picture is, of course, only one view of life in Mexico; but it is, fortunately, an important view, both for visitors and for the natives. However, like the United States, Mexico is made up of many different parts, some as modern as New York, some as old-fashioned as grandmother's trunk in a Vermont attic. Generally speaking, it is the cities of Mexico that are the most modern, cities like Mexico City, Guadalajara, and Monterey. Out in the country, things are still done in the old ways. This play takes place outside tiny San Marcos, a country village; but the people there know about the city. Some of them, like Licha, wish for the joys of the city. There are also people, of course, like Luisa, a city girl, who wish for the joys of the country. The songs, dances, and country customs of this play are all based on those still in use in Mexico today. For a general view of Mexico, Barbara Gomez's *Getting to Know Mexico* is recommended reading for young people. Music for the birthday morning song, *Las Mañanitas,* and some other versions of the lyrics may be found in Jarrett and McManus' *El Camino Real,* pp. 116-119.

Licha's Birthday Serenade

Characters

LICHA (*Alicia—Alice*), *a girl from the country*
PABLO (*Paul*), *her father*
MAMA, *her mother*
SERENADERS (*Mariachis*):
  MEMO (*Guillermo—William*)
  COCO (*Jorge—George*)
  PERICO (*Pedro—Peter*)
  PANCHO (*Francisco—Francis*)
  CHELA (*Graciela—Grace*)
  LOLA (*Dolores*)
  MARUCA (*Maria—Mary*)
  NITA (*Anita—Anne*)
LUISA (*Louise*), *a girl from the city*
SEÑOR HIDALGO, *her father*
SEÑORA HIDALGO, *her mother*

TIME: *The morning of Licha's birthday.*
SETTING: *The yard in front of Licha's adobe house.*
AT RISE: *The sun, a gold circle on a pole, rises in back of* LICHA'S *house and a rooster crows "cock-a-doodle-doo."* PABLO *comes out of the door, yawns and gives a wide stretch. The rooster crows again.*

PABLO: I heard you, Chanty. I heard you. I'm up. (*The* SERENADERS *or mariachis enter from downstage, the boys from the left and the girls from the right. Boys may carry musical instruments. Both boys and girls carry head masks of a funny male face, to be used later in the dance. The* SERENADERS *march to the center of the stage and then, two by two, they march upstage to the door of* LICHA's *house. As they march, they keep time by singing nonsense words: "Tra-la-la-la-la-la." When they reach the house, they part and line up in facing rows on each side of the door. They then sing the birthday morning song.*)

GIRLS: The nightingales were singing
On the day that you were born.

BOYS: Their song came softly winging
On the sunbeams of the morn.

GIRLS: They warbled a song of welcome,

BOYS: The same as we sing today—

ALL (*Together*): Wake up, wake up, little Licha,
And hear your birthday serenade.

PABLO (*Clapping*) Bravo! Bravo! That is a fine birthday song. Never have I heard you sing better, mariachis.

MEMO: But where is Licha? It is her song.

CHELA: Why does she not come out that we may wish her a happy birthday?

COCO: Has she not heard Chanty, the rooster, crow? Does she not know the sun is red in the sky?

LOLA: Does she not know her birthday has begun?

PABLO: Little Licha is, I think, afraid to wake up.

MARUCA: Afraid to wake up on her own birthday?

PERICO: On my birthday, I wake the rooster up.

PABLO: All night Licha has dreamed of a beautiful little

bracelet that she saw in a picture. And now she is afraid if she wakes up, the bracelet will be gone.

PANCHO: But Papa Pablo, why do you not wake her up and give her the bracelet?

NITA: That is what my papa did on my birthday when I got my little pearl necklace. Then I covered his face with kisses, and he told me that he was glad he woke me up.

PABLO: There is no bracelet to give Licha. You can get such a bracelet only in the city, and you must have money.

COCO: Don't you have money?

PERICO: Nobody in San Marcos has money this year.

CHELA: The tobacco did not grow.

MARUCA: And the bugs got the cotton.

PABLO: Sí, we have no money. But we have food and health and shelter and love. And these we will give Licha, and then she will be happy and laugh. (*Pause*) I hope.

NITA: You can get a *jicama* for her in the fields. She likes them when they are ripe and full of juice.

PABLO: She shall have one.

CHELA: And enchiladas, full of meat and rice and cheese, the way Licha's mama makes them.

PABLO: She shall have enchiladas, hot, with lots of meat. (*Laughs*) Indeed, why shouldn't she be happy? Who can be sad with enchiladas on the table? (*Stops*) But still she will not have her little bracelet, so maybe she will be sad even with enchiladas on the table. It is such a little thing, a bracelet. Any city girl would have five, but to Licha that little bracelet is bigger than the moon and brighter than the sun.

NITA: And when you are a girl and wish very hard for something and do not get it, it seems further away than the stars.

PANCHO: Maybe she will forget all about it. A girl wants one thing one day, and the next day she will tell you she never wanted it at all. My sister is like that, and she has been a girl for a long, long time. Maybe sixteen years.

NITA: Some girls want one thing, and they will want it forever. I was that way about my necklace.

PABLO: Well, we shall see, and hope for the best. (MAMA *comes out the door.*)

MAMA: The singing was pretty, mariachis.

MEMO: Is Licha awake?

LOLA: Did she hear her morning birthday serenade?

PABLO: Is our birthday girl yet awake, Mama?

MAMA: She is awake, but she has left her heart asleep in the land of dreams with her bracelet.

PABLO: I should have taken something to the city to sell. Then I could have bought Licha her bracelet.

MAMA: Don't blame yourself, Papa. You have nothing to sell that the city wants to buy. If she is supposed to get her bracelet on this birthday, she will get it. If not, there is always next year.

NITA: It won't be the same if she gets it next year. When a girl wishes for something very much and it does not happen, she becomes afraid ever to wish again.

MEMO: You are only *one* girl, Nita. How do you know what *every* girl wants?

NITA: And you are no girl at all, Memo. So you would never understand if I told you.

MEMO: Who wants to be a girl? I would not be a girl for all the bracelets in the world.

PABLO: Children, children. Come, come, let's have no more gloom. We are all here to make Licha happy on her birthday.

Coco: Yes, who cares about an old bracelet anyway?

MARUCA: We can make her happy without it.

PABLO: Yes, yes. Let us sing and laugh and dance and be happy.

PERICO: Let us do our *Dance of the Old Men* now.

CHELA: Yes, let us do the dance. That will make her laugh and be happy.

Coco (*Laughing*): It makes me laugh just to think about it and how she will laugh when she sees us.

MAMA (*Calling in the door*): Licha! Licha, come quickly. They are going to do *The Dance of the Old Men.*

PANCHO: If this does not make her laugh, she has no joy in her. (LICHA *comes out the door. She is very solemn.*)

ALL (*Together*): Happy Birthday, Licha.

LICHA: I want to thank all of you for coming to sing my birthday song and to wish me a happy day. (*Sighs*) And I will be happy even if I do not have my bracelet. I will be happy even if I am sad.

MAMA: If you are going to be happy, little Licha, you must smile a little. Just as the bean grows in the warm earth, so does happiness grow in a smiling face.

LOLA: We will make her smile.

MEMO: We will make her laugh so loud she will awaken the owls.

NITA: Well, let's put on masks and get started. But I know exactly how she feels. (*The* BOYS *gather in one group, the* GIRLS *in another; they all put on their masks. They all pretend to be very old and bent as they line up in opposing lines to start "The Dance of the Old Men." As they are getting in their positions,* LUISA *and her parents,* SEÑOR *and* SEÑORA HIDALGO, *enter downstage right.*)

LUISA (*Pointing at the dancers*): Look, Papa! Mama! They are going to have a dance. See, Papa, is not the country a wonderful place? All day they sing and dance and nobody has a worry about anything.

SEÑOR HIDALGO: All day they work in the country, just as we do in the city. I think maybe they worry a little here, too. This must be some special celebration, Luisa.

SEÑORA HIDALGO: See, Luisa, they are all dressed in their best clothes. People do not dress like that when they go to school or work in the fields any more in the country than we do in the city.

LUISA: Please, Papa, Mama. May we stay a bit and watch them? Just a few minutes? Because it is my birthday?

SEÑOR HIDALGO (*Laughing*): Sí, Luisa. For a few minutes. Because it is your birthday.

SEÑORA HIDALGO: Papa and I will do what you wish all day, Luisa, for this has been your birthday wish—to spend the day in the country. If you want to stay and watch, we will stay and watch.

LUISA: Look, they are starting. It is a dance. ("*The Dance of the Old Men" begins. The dancers all sing and beat time with their feet. Then one couple at a time skip out to meet each other; when they meet, they do a heel-toe step. Then each steps back to bow to the other. As they do, each grabs his back as though it has been strained by the dancing and bowing and then hobbles and limps back to the line; and the next couple comes out. As the dancing is going on, the* SERENADERS *sing*):

ALL (*Singing*): I love to dance
With a love that does not tire;
So now we dance,
As in youth we did desire.
And though our bones are stiff
As seasoned timber,
We dance the same as we did
When we were young and limber.

CHORUS: Oh, we are old men,
But you would never know it.
We are old men,
But you would never know it.
We are old men,
But look at the way we toe it:
Heel. Toe. Heel. Toe.
Look at the way we toe it.
(*All grabbing their backs in unison*) But, oh, our aching backs. Hah! (*The dancers take off their masks and throw their arms in the air. They all laugh.*)

LUISA (*Clapping her hands*): Wonderful! Wonderful!

SEÑOR HIDALGO (*Applauding*): Bravo! Bravo! (The SERE-NADERS *turn downstage to look at the visitors. Going to them with* SEÑORA HIDALGO *and* LUISA) Our pardon, we did not mean to interrupt.

PABLO: It is no interruption, Señor. Today is our Licha's birthday, and some of her friends came to serenade her and to dance *The Dance of the Old Men* for her.

LUISA: Imagine that. A serenade all her own for her birthday. See, Papa, it is as I have said: the country is a wonderful place to live.

NITA: Do you live in the city?

SEÑOR HIDALGO: Sí, I am Señor Hidalgo. And this is my wife and our little girl, Luisa. We live in Guadalajara.

MEMO: Guadalajara! Imagine that.

CHELA: Teacher says that Guadalajara is the second largest city in all of Mexico. Why, a single street there is bigger than all of our San Marcos.

LICHA: To live in the city is a dream. Everything there must be like paradise.

SEÑOR HIDALGO (*Laughing*): You see, Luisa, some people would like to live in the city. (*To* PABLO) My little girl thinks that it would be wonderful to live in the country all the time. She thinks people are happy only in the country.

PABLO (*Laughing*): Sí, Señor. It is always the same. For the young, the grass is always greener—yes, and sweeter, too—on another hill.

SEÑOR HIDALGO: All year Luisa has been telling her mother and me that for her birthday she wanted nothing but to spend the whole day in the country. So that is why we are here today. It is Luisa's birthday present.

PERICO: It is her birthday?

MARUCA: Then we shall have to sing a birthday morning song for Luisa, too. (*To* LUISA) May we sing our serenade for your birthday, Luisa?

LUISA: Would you really? I would like that very much. Papa, Mama, I am to have a serenade for my birthday. Listen. (*The* SERENADERS *sing "The Birthday Morning Song" to* LUISA. *It is the same song, but this time they use her name instead of* LICHA's.) Oh, thank you. Thank you. My own birthday song. The girls at my school will not believe it when I tell them what has happened to me on my birthday. First I see *The Dance of the Old Men,* and then I am serenaded. See, Papa, did I not tell you that miracles happen every day in the country?

MAMA: Señora Hidalgo, my family would be very pleased if you and your family would stay and share our birthday celebrations with us.

PABLO: We are just having enchiladas.

NITA: But they have lots of chicken in them.

SEÑOR HIDALGO: You have all been very kind to us, but we cannot impose upon you. After all, we are only strangers passing by.

PABLO: In the country, Señor Hidalgo, there are no strangers. Just relatives, neighbors, and friends. (*Laughs*) Sometimes one may be all three. But since you are not a relative or neighbor, you must be a friend. (*Stops*) But, of course, if you do not think you would like Mama's enchiladas. . . .

SEÑOR HIDALGO: If you want us, Señor, we will stay. Best of all things in life is to eat enchiladas. I live in the city, my friend, but I am not a foreigner. I know what is good to eat. Thank you, my friend. I love enchiladas.

NITA: Especially with lots of chicken in them.

PABLO: Then it is settled, Señor. Everybody is staying. (*He bows and waves them all to enter the house.*) *Aqui tiene su casa!* My house is yours!

LUISA (*Gives a cry of alarm*): Oh, Papa, I just thought. We have no present for Licha's birthday.

PABLO: A smile and a warm heart is all the present needed.

LUISA (*Taking a box from her pocket*): But, wait! I do

have something. May I, Mama? May I give Licha . . . ?

SEÑORA HIDALGO (*Laughing*): The present from Uncle Guillermo? Yes, Luisa, you may.

LUISA (*Going to* LICHA): Licha, I wish to make you a birthday presentation, but first I must explain.

LICHA: You do not need to give me a present, Luisa. As Papa says, it is a great present to me that you have come to our house.

LUISA: But I want to give you a present. And I must explain why I wish to give you *this* present. In Mexico City lives my uncle, Guillermo.

NITA: In Mexico City. Imagine that.

LUISA: And in Monterey lives my Aunt Graciela.

CHELA: Graciela. That is my name, too. But everyone calls me Chela.

LUISA: And each year, Uncle Guillermo and Aunt Graciela send me presents. But they always send the same thing. And although I always like their presents very much, I never need two. This year both sent me this. (*Hands her the box*) I like mine very much, and I hope you will like yours, too. It will make me very happy if you take it.

LICHA (*Taking the box*): I thank you very much, Luisa. And I thank your Uncle Guillermo in Mexico City and your Aunt Graciela in Monterey, too.

NITA: What is it, Licha? Let us see it. Hold it up.

LICHA: It's . . . It is . . . (*She holds it up.*) It is my silver bracelet! The very one I saw in the picture. (*Hugs* LUISA) Thank you, Luisa. Thank you. This is the happiest birthday in my whole life.

COCO: Now that Licha's birthday dream has come true

and she will smile all year, let's sing a serenade to the two birthday girls.

PERICO: And make it twice as loud, for there are two of them.

PABLO: Let the celebration start and let's sing and laugh and dance and eat until the sun goes down and the moon comes up.

MAMA: And maybe a little after. (*The families start into the house. The* SERENADERS *sing the birthday song. While they are singing, the stage lights dim. The sun goes down, and the moon—a silver foil crescent attached to a pole—rises. A single spotlight shines on the moon as the curtain falls.*)

THE END

THE GOLDEN VOICE OF LITTLE ERIK
(*Norway*)

Author's Notes on THE GOLDEN VOICE OF LITTLE ERIK

The people of Norway know that life can be full of hardship. They have learned this from their country's rigorous climate, from their hazardous occupations, and from the wars that have been fought on the borders of their peaceful land. But they also know what it is to dream, and in their folk tales these dreams are revealed.

This play, "The Golden Voice of Little Erik," is based upon one of the Norwegian folk tales of Jorgen Moe and Peter Asbjörnsen. It illustrates three things about the Norwegian: his sense of the difficulty of life, his ability to find hope in his dreams, and his unfailing sense of humor.

The Golden Voice of Little Erik

Characters

LITTLE ERIK

SHERIFF

FIRST BEGGAR, *an old woman*

SECOND BEGGAR, *an old man*

THIRD BEGGAR, *a little girl*

CLOTHING MERCHANT

CHRISTINA, *his daughter*

TWO GUARDS

TOWNSPEOPLE

SETTING: *A street in Norway. A jail may be seen in the background. In front of it is a wooden bench.*

AT RISE: LITTLE ERIK *is sweeping the street and singing.*

ERIK (*Singing, off-key, to the tune of Edvard Grieg's "Norwegian Dance #2"*)

> The sun is bright, the world is gay,
> Children sing as merrily they play,
> That's the way I think the world ought to be,
> Full of fun and full of joy and melody;
> The world is oh so jolly, lovely as can be,
> With beauty everywhere for me to see.

(SHERIFF *enters from right, and struts over to* ERIK.)

SHERIFF: Ah, the happy days of youth. It is too bad you have such a horrible voice.

151

ERIK: My voice might be better, Sheriff, if I ate more often.

SHERIFF: Come, come. Don't complain. Your three years of apprenticeship to me are up, and now you can see if the rest of Norway will treat you as well as I have.

ERIK: (*Putting the broom against the jail wall*): If it does, I shall die thin.

SHERIFF: Now, Erik, I fed you as I promised your father I would when he apprenticed you to me three years ago.

ERIK: Aye, that you did, but only what the prisoners refused to eat.

SHERIFF: Prisoners are all hard to please.

ERIK: And you promised me shelter, and many a cold night I slept on the floor without even a blanket.

SHERIFF: I was doing you a favor, Erik. Your next work may be in Lofoden or even Hammerfest, and you'll thank me then for preparing you for the real cold.

ERIK: And you promised me clothes.

SHERIFF: And what are you wearing? Lilies?

ERIK: They are sad-looking lilies if they are. You know right well these are the same clothes I brought with me three years ago.

SHERIFF: I hate to hear a man complain. It promises nothing but trouble for his future.

ERIK: I do not mean to complain, sir, but sometimes it seems to me that my last three years would have been easier if I had been your prisoner rather than your apprentice.

SHERIFF: Ho, ho. That's a funny one. I must tell it to the Mayor. I am glad you have kept your sense of humor,

Erik. It may get you out of many a scrape that your complaining will get you into.

ERIK: Well, this is an odd world. Or at least, it is in Norway. When I state the facts, I am accused of either complaining or joking. And the truth of the matter is that I feel neither like laughing nor crying, but just like stretching my legs and singing a song.

SHERIFF: Just let that singing go for now. At least until I am out of the sound of that awful voice of yours. (*Takes purse from his belt*) Now, lad, here comes your pay. Hold out your hand.

ERIK: Aye, this I have been waiting for. Now I shall buy myself some clothes and have myself a fine meal.

SHERIFF (*Counting as he drops the coins into* ERIK'S *hand*): One. Two. Three. There you are, boy. Three pennies.

ERIK: Three pennies for three years? Is that my pay?

SHERIFF: Aye, lad, have you ever had so much money in all your life before?

ERIK: Since I have never had any money before, it is more than I have ever had. But three pennies for three years of work doesn't seem like very much.

SHERIFF: There you go with your complaining again. You complain about everything: the cold, the hardness of the floor, the food you eat, the clothes you don't have. And now you complain abut your pay. There's no pleasing you, boy. And all of your complaining has quite ruined my appetite. I'm sure I shan't be able to eat a bite of the delicious banquet the Mayor is having today. (*He turns and starts off right.*)

ERIK: If it will make you happy, I'll be glad to go to the

Mayor's with you and eat your meal. Just so that no food will be wasted, I mean.

SHERIFF: Insolent boy! I shall eat every bite and probably ask for extras, although it will probably make me ill. (*To audience*) Why do the poor complain so much? It doesn't help them at all, and it makes life so unpleasant for the rest of us. (SHERIFF *exits.*)

ERIK: The sheriff is right. I really shouldn't complain. I have three pennies, and the world is all before me. (*He starts off left, singing, "The sun is bright, etc., etc." FIRST BEGGAR enters left and stops him.*)

FIRST BEGGAR: You seem happy, boy, even if your singing sounds like a cat that swallowed a fishbone.

ERIK: Oh, I am, Old Mother. I have three pennies and the world is all before me.

FIRST BEGGAR: Give me a penny, for I am old and hungry, and the world is all behind me.

ERIK: I had planned to buy some clothes.

FIRST BEGGAR: Your clothes are better than mine, and also I am hungry.

ERIK: Indeed my clothes are better, Old Mother. All right, here's a penny, and may good fortune find you.

FIRST BEGGAR: You are a good boy, even if you have a terrible voice, and you will be rewarded. (*She goes across stage right and exits.*)

ERIK: I haven't taken a dozen steps, and I am already a penny poorer. At this rate, I'd have to be a millionaire to cross from Bergen to Oslo. Oh, well, I still have two pennies, and the world is still before me. (*Starts singing, still off-key, "The sun is bright," etc., etc. SECOND BEGGAR enters from left, leaning on a staff or cane.*)

SECOND BEGGAR: Young man, you don't sing very well.

ERIK: Indeed I don't, Old Father, or so everybody tells me. And it's a pity, too, for I would like to sing so gaily that all the world would like my song as well as I do. But I mean well, Old Father.

SECOND BEGGAR: Do you indeed? Then give me a penny so that I may eat, for I have not tasted so much as a corner of a crumb since noon yesterday.

ERIK: I am indeed sorry, Old Father, but I have but two pennies in all the world, and I need to buy some clothes.

SECOND BEGGAR: Your clothes are better than mine, and your hunger not so great.

ERIK: That's true, Old Father. Here's the penny.

SECOND BEGGAR: Thank you, my son. You're a good boy even if you have a horrible voice, and you shall be rewarded. (*He crosses stage right and exits.*)

ERIK: Indeed, I am probably a very foolish boy, as the sheriff has often told me. But I'd rather have a hard knot in my stomach from hunger than a hard knot in my heart from meanness. And besides, I still have a penny, and the world is all before me. (*He starts to sing as before, and the* THIRD BEGGAR *comes in from left and pulls at his shirt.*) Oh, oh. I *had* a penny. There's no sense in arguing about it, for I shall give it to her in the long run, anyway. (*Gives her his last penny*) Here you are, Little Sister. It won't buy much, but it may help. (THIRD BEGGAR *looks up at him.*) No, don't thank me. I know what you will say. I have been a good boy, and I will be rewarded. (THIRD BEGGAR *nods and starts off right.*) Now I am certain of one thing—the next beggar will get nothing from me, for I have now nothing to give.

THIRD BEGGAR (*Stopping just before she exits at stage*

right and turning): Goodbye, Little Brother. And you will be rewarded! (*Exits right*)

ERIK (*Laughing*): No pennies have I to worry me now, but the world is still before me so I might as well sing and be happy. (*Starts singing, "The sun is bright," etc., etc.* FIRST BEGGAR *enters from stage left again.* ERIK *takes a quick look at her, a quick look stage right and then speaks to her.*) My goodness, you either have a twin sister, or you have circled the world in a hurry.

FIRST BEGGAR: I have returned to you because you are a good boy.

ERIK: I thank you, Old Mother. But I have no more pennies.

FIRST BEGGAR: I know. I saw you give all you had away. That's why I have returned. For every penny you gave, I now give you a wish. Three pennies. Three wishes.

ERIK: My goodness, again. This often happens in the world I see with my eyes closed, but never before in the world I see with my eyes open.

FIRST BEGGAR: It is happening now, so wish and wish well.

ERIK: First, I wish that I could sing so well that everyone who heard me would want to dance.

FIRST BEGGAR: That's a foolish wish. But think and wish again.

ERIK: Then I wish that everyone who danced would be happy.

FIRST BEGGAR: That's more foolish than the first. Now think carefully before you wish again.

ERIK: And then, for my third wish, I wish that all the people made happy by my singing and their dancing would like me so much that they would give me whatever I needed without my ever asking.

FIRST BEGGAR: There may be wisdom in your foolishness. At least, we can wait and see. Your wishes are granted, and good fortune, my son. (FIRST BEGGAR *exits left*.)

ERIK: I suppose it's either a dream or a joke. It's always one or the other whenever anything good looks as if it's about to happen to me. But I'll try it. (*Sings, for the first time on key*)

> The sun is bright, the world is gay,
> Children sing as in the spring they play;
> That's the way I think the world ought to be,
> Full of fun and full of joy and melody.
> The world is oh so jolly, lovely as can be
> With beauty everywhere for me to see!

My goodness! I do sing better, or at least it sounds better to me. (*Enter* MERCHANT *with his daughter,* CHRISTINA, *from left. He carries a bag.*) And the world is beautiful. Even with my eyes open now. (*Starts singing again, "The sun is bright," etc., etc.*)

CHRISTINA: Oh, Father, stop and dance with me. That boy's singing just makes my feet go jumping.

MERCHANT: It is most ridiculous, but I feel the same way, Christina. (MERCHANT *puts down his bag, takes* CHRISTINA's *hand, and they dance a brief country dance, as* ERIK *hums and sings.*)

ERIK (*Stops singing*): My goodness. My singing *does* make people dance.

CHRISTINA: Indeed it does. It makes me happy, too. Oh, Father, I don't know when I have ever been so happy before.

MERCHANT: I'm so happy, I'm giddy. But tell me, young

man, what is a boy with such a fine voice doing with such old clothes?

ERIK: They are all I have. I had three pennies to buy more, but I gave them away.

CHRISTINA: Oh, Father, give him some of the clothes from your bag.

MERCHANT: I've never done such a thing before, but I don't know why I shouldn't. Indeed I shall. (*He takes the bag, opens it, and draws out a plumed hat, a silk blouse, trousers, and a cloak. He gives them to* ERIK, *who draws them on over his rags.*)

ERIK: My wishes have come true. People dance to my singing, and their dancing makes them happy. And happy people, it seems, are generous ones, too. The world is really a happy, jolly place—at least it is for me.

CHRISTINA: Oh, Father, doesn't he look handsome?

MERCHANT: Indeed he does, and indeed he should, for not even the sheriff dresses so well. But come, Christina, we must go. I have business in the village.

CHRISTINA: Oh, Father, must we go? I would like to stay and dance.

MERCHANT: I would, too. But we shall return later and listen more to this boy's golden voice.

ERIK: A golden voice! That sounds very nice: the golden voice of Erik.

CHRISTINA: The golden voice of *little* Erik.

ERIK: I am not so little now that I have a fine hat. But I thank you, merchant. And I thank you, Christina.

MERCHANT (*Starting off left with* CHRISTINA): Goodbye. Goodbye, we shall return for more singing and dancing and laughter, by and by. (*Exit right.*)

ERIK: Here I am with fine clothes and a fine voice. It

has been less than an hour since I left the sheriff's employment, and I am already living in a bright new world. And what tomorrow brings only my good fairies know. But I might as well sit down and rest, for the merchant and his daughter will return, and I must sing them another song in payment for the fine clothes they have given me. (ERIK *sits down, and* SHERIFF *enters from right.*)

SHERIFF: Sitting down, Erik? You haven't traveled much since we parted company.

ERIK (*Rising*): No, sir, but I have yet seen much of the world I never knew before.

SHERIFF: But what's this? What's this you're wearing? Where did you steal these clothes, boy?

ERIK: I didn't steal them, sir. A merchant gave them to me.

SHERIFF: Nonsense. No merchant ever gave anything to any beggar, and you couldn't even buy the ribbon on your hat for three pennies, so don't tell me you bought them.

ERIK: No, sir. I didn't buy them. He gave them to me because he liked my singing. He and his daughter both liked it. They said I had a golden voice.

SHERIFF: That's the most miserable lie I ever heard. He may have beaten you on the head for your singing, but to give you clothes, never.

ERIK: But I sing well now. I'll show you. Listen.

SHERIFF: If you utter a note, I shall strike you on the head. (*Shouting*) Guards! Guards! Come here at once! I've caught a thief. (*Enter* TWO GUARDS *running, followed by some* TOWNSPEOPLE.) Take this fellow and throw him in jail. He's a thief.

FIRST GUARD: But that's little Erik, your apprentice.

SHERIFF: Not any more! He has stolen these clothes, and he has the impudence to tell me that a merchant gave them to him—a merchant who *liked* his singing.

SECOND GUARD: He proved his own guilt by that statement, for I have heard him sing. (*Tries to take* ERIK *by the arm*) Now, come along, Erik.

FIRST GUARD: And if you behave yourself, you may be out again in ninety-nine years. (ERIK *pulls away from the* GUARDS *and talks to the* TOWNSPEOPLE.)

ERIK: But you must listen to me. It's true. A merchant gave me these clothes because my singing made him happy.

FIRST PERSON: Who ever heard of such a thing?

SECOND PERSON: Erik's singing makes me sad.

THIRD PERSON: It makes me ill.

ERIK: You must listen. He said I had a golden voice, and he is going to return to listen some more.

FIRST PERSON: Ho, ho. A golden voice! How ridiculous!

SECOND PERSON: He may have given you the clothes to bribe you to be quiet. (FIRST BEGGAR *enters from right.*)

FIRST BEGGAR: Why not give the boy a chance? Let him sing.

THIRD TOWNSPERSON: Who are you?

FIRST BEGGAR: A stranger.

FIRST TOWNSPERSON: Anyone would know that, for little Erik has the worst voice that ever was. (SECOND BEGGAR *enters from right.*)

SECOND BEGGAR: I say let little Erik sing.

FIRST TOWNSPERSON: Oh, all right, let him sing, and then send him to jail for his bad singing. It will save time.

ERIK (*Starting to sing to tune of Edvard Grieg's "Norwegian Dance #2"*)

From sky to sea, from earth to moon,
The world is full of every kind of beauty;
As I look around me, I can see
The world is full of music and jollity;
With rolling hills and valleys, lovely as can be,
It makes my heart so gay, I'm full of joy and glee.

(TOWNSPEOPLE *start to dance.*)

ERIK: See, I told you. My voice has changed.

SECOND TOWNSPERSON: Oh, sing some more. We want to dance.

ERIK: Now do you believe me?

FIRST TOWNSPERSON: Yes, we believe you, but sing!

ERIK: And you won't let the sheriff send me to jail?

FIRST TOWNSPERSON: Indeed not. We'll make you the sheriff.

SECOND TOWNSPERSON: The sheriff can be your apprentice for three years.

ERIK: Sheriff, what do you say to that?

SHERIFF: You the sheriff and me the apprentice? Well, now, let's see. All right, that's fine with me. Now sing, sing, sing! I want to dance, too. (*He jumps in the air. LITTLE ERIK starts singing; everyone begins to dance and to join in the singing as the curtain falls.*)

THE END

STANISLAW AND THE WOLF
(Poland)

Author's Notes on STANISLAW AND THE WOLF

During much of its history, Poland has existed in a state of "legalized anarchy," as a herd of sheep surrounded by hungry wolves. Most of the strong military powers of Europe have, at one time or another, made their camps in this north-central European nation—the French under Napoleon, the Russians under Catherine, the Germans under Hitler, and now the Soviets. It is not surprising, therefore, that the folk tales of the Poles are frequently grim and that even the Polish saints, like Stanislaw, are as much respected for their cunning in "fooling the wolf" as they are for their goodness in "feeding the lamb."

The folk legend upon which this play is based is set in the Golden Age of Poland, when animals could talk and men like St. Stanislaw lived in peaceful communion with them. But even in this Golden Age, there were the wolves, ready to pounce on man and devour him.

Stanislaw and the Wolf

Characters

St. Stanislaw, *patron saint of Poland*
Ivan, *the bear*
Sam, *the squirrel*
Masha, *the rabbit*
Andrey, *the fox*
Adolph, *the wolf*
Roddey, *a schoolboy*
Bertha, *an old woman*
Walter, *the blacksmith*

Time: *Long, long ago.*
Setting: *A clearing in the woods, in front of the hut of St. Stanislaw.*
At Rise: St. Stanislaw *is sitting in front of his hut. With a flat stone, he is grinding wheat into flour in an earthen bowl. Off-stage can be heard the singing of birds.*

Stanislaw: The birds are in the trees, the air is free, and the water flows clear in the rippling brook. It's easy to see all's right with the world. (Ivan, *the bear, comes running in yelling and holding his nose with both paws.*) My goodness! All's not right with my friend,

165

Ivan, the bear. (*To* Ivan, *rising*) What has happened, my friend? Did Mrs. Bear poke you on the nose?

Ivan: Indeed not. It's the miserable bees. They stung me again—and for nothing.

Stanislaw: For nothing? I'll have to speak to them about it.

Ivan: Well, *almost* for nothing. I was just going to taste a *little* honey.

Stanislaw: Ivan, my friend. My friend, Ivan. When will you learn to keep your nose out of the beehive? It seems to me that you get it stung at least once a week.

Ivan: I know. I know, and it hurts so. But what am I to do? I love honey so much that I can't keep away from it.

Stanislaw: Unless one learns to like only those things that are his, he may expect many a sharp pain in this life. When, oh when will all my friends learn there is enough for everyone in this world without robbing our neighbors?

Ivan: You are right and good, Brother Stanislaw. Of course, it is easy to be right if one is good. But if it's all the same to you, I'll take the sermon later. Now, tell me what to do about my nose.

Stanislaw: Go to the river bank and put mud on your nose, and sit quietly and stay away from bees.

Ivan: I shall, Brother Stanislaw. I shall. Thank you. (Ivan *exits*.)

Stanislaw: And he will, too, until the next time. I should keep a supply of wet mud here just for Ivan. He'll always need it. (Sam *and* Masha *enter, holding hands and laughing*.) Hello, my friends. It is good to see that joy and laughter have not disappeared from this world.

SAM: Good morning, Brother Stanislaw.

MASHA: Good morning, Brother Stanislaw.

STANISLAW: Tell me, why are you so happy? Because it is spring?

SAM: Well, yes, partly.

STANISLAW: Because the birds are singing?

MASHA: Yes, that, too.

STANISLAW: Because the water in the brook is clear?

SAM: I guess because of that, too.

STANISLAW: Because all's right with the world?

MASHA: Oh, that most of all. Do you know what we did? (*Laughs*) You tell him, Sam.

SAM: No, you tell him, Masha.

MASHA: Oh, you tell him.

SAM: You tell it better than I do. Girls always do.

MASHA: But this is the sort of thing a boy tells better.

STANISLAW: Will *one* of you please tell me?

MASHA: All right, I'll tell you. You know Andrey, the fox?

STANISLAW: Indeed I do.

SAM: She has a garden full of the most wonderful things: nuts and carrots and . . .

MASHA: I thought I was going to tell this.

SAM (*Bowing from the waist*): My pardon, madam—after you.

MASHA: Early this morning when Andrey was working in her garden, we sent Sandra Sparrow to tell her that in the west end of the forest there grew carrots as big as trees.

SAM: And when she went to get some, we jumped into her garden and ate and ate and ate.

MASHA: I thought I was going to tell this!

SAM: Again my pardon, madam—after you.

MASHA: Everything tasted so good—the carrots and lettuce especially!

SAM: And the nuts were delicious. (*To* MASHA) If I may be permitted to interrupt to say so?

STANISLAW: My goodness, you two are going to have trouble when Andrey returns. She won't like this.

SAM: We know. We hid in the bushes until she returned.

MASHA: Her face grew blue and then purple and then green. It was the funniest thing.

STANISLAW: I am disappointed in both of you. The forest is full of things that you may eat. Why must you take things that don't belong to you?

MASHA: They taste so much better in Andrey's garden than in the woods.

STANISLAW: You are both being very foolish. There will be trouble for you, I'm afraid.

SAM: Oh, Brother Stanislaw, laugh with us, and don't give us a sermon on a full stomach.

MASHA: Indeed, one should be in pain when listening to a sermon.

STANISLAW: Ivan did not think so, but perhaps it is different with you two. At least we will have a chance to find out, for here comes Andrey now.

SAM: Oh! We must run. Don't tell her where we are. (*Starts off running*)

MASHA: Sam, Sam, wait for me!

SAM: Not this time. This time, it's after *me,* madam. (*He runs off right and she follows.*)

STANISLAW: With so much good in this world, why do all my friends find so much bad to do? (ANDREY *enters, bent over sniffing the ground.* STANISLAW *takes a pinch of something from his pocket and throws it in* ANDREY'S *face.*) Oh, excuse me, friend Andrey.

ANDREY (*Sneezing*): Pepper! Dear me, I've lost my sense of smell. Now I shall never find them.

STANISLAW: Never find whom?

ANDREY: Sam and Masha. They sent me on a fool's errand this morning, and while I was gone they robbed my garden.

STANISLAW: That wasn't a very nice thing to do. But perhaps it is just as well that you don't find them now until you calm down. You wouldn't want to do anything you'd be sorry for.

ANDREY: *I'm* not going to be sorry. *They* are. I'm going to eat them.

STANISLAW: Dear me, now you are talking like Adolph the wolf.

ANDREY: That's the way I'm going to be from now on. No more vegetables and salads for me. From now on, I'm going to eat meat.

STANISLAW: Oh, dear, oh, dear, oh dear. What is happening to the forest? Soon no creature will be safe from any other creature.

ANDREY: I don't care. They started it, and besides I think that tender rabbit and squirrel will taste just fine. Do you know where they are, Brother Stanislaw?

STANISLAW: Not exactly. But I think you will be wise if you go in that direction. (*Points off left, the opposite direction from that of* SAM *and* MASHA) Yes, I think you will be wise if you go that way.

ANDREY: Thank you, Brother Stanislaw. And if I catch them, you must come for dinner.

STANISLAW: I liked your dinners of greens, Andrey. But I don't think I should care to eat my friends, or soon my friends might care to eat me.

ANDREY: Suit yourself. But the way things are going these days, they may anyway. Thank you for your advice, Brother Stanislaw. This way you say?

STANISLAW: I think that would be the wise way to go. (ANDREY *exits.*) Oh, dear, oh dear, oh dear. That was almost a lie. But I do believe that she is wise to go in the opposite direction. Perhaps when she thinks about it some more, Sister Andrey will give Sam and Masha another chance. I certainly hope so. How can things be so right with the world and so wrong with all my friends? It is something I must think about. (ADOLPH, *the wolf, enters.*)

ADOLPH: Good morning, Brother Stanislaw.

STANISLAW: Good morning, Adolph.

ADOLPH: What are you doing?

STANISLAW: Thinking.

ADOLPH: Thinking? What on earth for?

STANISLAW: I was wondering why, when this world has so much good to offer, all my friends hunger after bad.

ADOLPH: I'm glad you mentioned that.

STANISLAW: You are? I'm pleased that you are concerned with the state of the world. I must admit, Brother Adolph, that I had just about given you up for lost. Tell me, why do you think we all ignore the good and look for the bad?

ADOLPH: I wasn't talking about that. I was talking about hunger. I'm hungry.

STANISLAW: There are many fruits in the forest, and I am making some bread which I will share with you.

ADOLPH: I'm hungry. I want meat!

STANISLAW: Do you think it right for the strong to live off the weak?

ADOLPH: I shouldn't live at all if I tried to live off the strong. But don't have any worries for your little friends. I am not hungry for rabbit or squirrel.

STANISLAW: I'm glad to hear that, at least. Ivan is at the river bank, if you were thinking of trying bear.

ADOLPH: I'm not such a fool as that. Besides bear meat is tough. My friend, Nito the Weasel, has told me about the tenderest meat in the world.

STANISLAW: Nito! You are not keeping very good company, Adolph.

ADOLPH: He says it's man.

STANISLAW: My goodness, you are not thinking of eating a man!

ADOLPH: As a matter of fact, I am. And don't try to talk me out of it with any of your sermons. I just want to know one thing.

STANISLAW: Man. My goodness. Nito has certainly deceived you. Man is the toughest meat of all.

ADOLPH: I don't mean to question your word, Brother Stanislaw, but I think I'll find out for myself. I was just wondering if you had any suggestions as to what kind of man might taste best.

STANISLAW: Believe me, none of them tastes good. But let me warn you: don't eat any little boys on their way to school. They taste simply terrible.

ADOLPH: All little boys?

STANISLAW: All little boys, without exception. And don't eat any old ladies on their way to market. They are tough and stringy and all pepper and salt.

ADOLPH: No little boys on their way to school and no old ladies on their way to market. All right. Now tell me what *should* I eat.

STANISLAW: The tenderest of all men—and even he's not very tender—is the blacksmith. He works by a fire all day, and this keeps his flesh soft and tender.

ADOLPH: A blacksmith. I'll remember that, and I'll eat no other except a blacksmith. For my first try, that is. Of course, if I find blacksmith meat good, I may later try others—even boys on their way to school and old ladies on their way to market.

STANISLAW: I think that's sensible. Try the blacksmith first.

ADOLPH: Yes, indeed. One must be so careful in trying something new. First impressions are so lasting.

STANISLAW (*Taking his bowl*): Now, if you don't mind, I must go into the house and bake my bread.

ADOLPH (*Sitting down*): You don't mind if I wait here for a blacksmith, do you?

STANISLAW: No, be my guest. But don't forget—be sure it's a blacksmith.

ADOLPH: Oh, I'll be sure. I'll ask him. (STANISLAW *goes into house.* ADOLPH, *singing*) As I was sitting all alone, who should come up to me—a jolly, rosy blacksmith man, as tasty as could be. (RODDEY *enters with books strapped together over his shoulder.* ADOLPH, *rising*) Hello there, my friend. Are you a blacksmith?

RODDEY: Of course not. Can't you see my books? I'm a school boy on his way to school.

ADOLPH: Of course! You do look unappetizing. Well, on your way. I'm waiting for a blacksmith. (RODDEY *exits.* ADOLPH *sitting down again*) I'm certainly thankful to

Brother Stanislaw for warning me about eating boys on their way to school. I had a feeling that even one bite out of that hide would make my stomach ache all night. (BERTHA *enters, carrying a market basket.* ADOLPH, *rising*) Hello, there, my friend. Are you a blacksmith?

BERTHA: That's a very silly question to ask. Don't you see my market basket?

ADOLPH: I don't like people who answer questions by asking questions. Are you or are you not a blacksmith?

BERTHA: Indeed I am not. I am an old lady on her way to the market.

ADOLPH: I should have guessed. All tough and stringy and pepper and salt. Well, on your way. I'm waiting for a blacksmith.

BERTHA (*Shaking her head and marching off*): You're not very polite.

ADOLPH (*Yelling after her*): I don't have to be polite. I'm a wolf. (*She exits and he sits down.*) Polite! If she thinks I'm going to eat something tough and stringy and full of salt and pepper just to be polite, she has another guess coming. In fact, if a blacksmith doesn't come along soon, I might just give up the idea of eating any man. People, it seems, are very inconsiderate. (WALTER, *the blacksmith, enters. He wears a black apron.* ADOLPH, *without rising*) Are you, by any chance, a blacksmith?

WALTER: Why yes, Brother Wolf, I am. Can I do anything for you?

ADOLPH (*Jumping up*): You are! Good. I am going to eat you.

WALTER: Oh, you are? That's interesting.

ADOLPH: Yes, indeed I am. I told Brother Stanislaw that

I wanted to eat man, and he told me that the tenderest of all men was the blacksmith.

WALTER: I'll try to see that I don't disappoint that good old man. But first let me go to the creek and wash my face and hands. I wouldn't want to spoil your dinner with dust.

ADOLPH: All right. (WALTER *goes upstage left and takes a huge club from under a bush. He swings it a few times for practice.* ADOLPH *takes out a huge white napkin and ties it around his neck.*)

WALTER (*Putting the club behind his back and coming downstage to* ADOLPH): Well, I am all ready, except that my hands are wet. Let me dry them on your bushy tail.

ADOLPH: I don't really like getting my tail wet. But all right. Just this once. (*He turns around and bends over.* WALTER *grabs him by the tail with one hand and beats him on the head with his club.* ADOLPH *leaps and jumps and yells, then falls flat on the ground.* STANISLAW *comes out of the house.*)

STANISLAW: Well, Mr. Blacksmith, has Adolph finished his dinner?

WALTER: He's finished it, but I think he has lost his taste for man.

STANISLAW: I hope so, Walter. I hope so. I feel sorry for the poor fellow there, but he who won't learn by one man's kindness will eventually learn by another man's club. It's a hard lesson, though.

WALTER: It is indeed. But I must be on my way.

STANISLAW: May I have your apron, Brother Walter? Perhaps Adolph hasn't had his fill of blacksmith yet, and he might like your apron for dessert.

WALTER (*Laughing and taking off the apron and throw-*

ing it to STANISLAW): I have a whole shop full of hammers if Adolph wants an after-dinner mint. (WALTER *exits.*)

STANISLAW (*Shaking* ADOLPH): Adolph, Adolph, wake up! Wake up!

ADOLPH (*Sitting up*): What happened? What happened?

STANISLAW: That's what I was going to ask you. When I came out I found you here like this.

ADOLPH: I think I ate a blacksmith. At least I started to.

STANISLAW (*Handing him the apron*): Then this must be left over from your meal. Do you want to eat it now?

ADOLPH (*Jumping up*): Good heavens, no! That was the toughest meat I ever ate. In fact, I think I will see Andrey, the fox, about helping her tend her garden. I don't think I ever want to eat meat again. (*Limps off, shaking his head. As he reaches exit, he turns.*) The taste is all right—but it's so hard on the digestion! (*Quick curtain*)

THE END

THE HIGHLAND FLING

(*Scotland*)

Author's Notes on THE HIGHLAND FLING

Scotland has had a stormy history. For almost a thousand years, it was the favorite place for an invasion by the hardy Norsemen. It has been, moreover, a land of fierce clan wars, the Campbells against the O'Shanters; the Sinclairs against the MacAlisters; the Lauders against the MacDonalds. Scotland is a land in which even nature has taken a hand in molding a hardy people. The hills and rolling plains developed strong legs; the bitter cold, wet winters developed stout hearts. The Scotch, however, love everything about their land, perhaps most of all the hard life. In their songs they sing about the land of the mist and the storm, of the snow and the lightning, of the fierce battles. Their dances, too, are celebrations of the vigorous life. People who enjoy strenuous dances like the Sword Dance, the Highland Fling, and the Scotch Reel are people to whom dancing is no soft, gentle thing. The Scotch do not dance only for fun; they dance, also, for victory and to show their physical prowess. This play is based on an episode that the writer Robert Louis Stevenson saw when he was visiting Scotland a century ago.

The Highland Fling

Characters

GARTY MACALISTER   ELLISON CAMPBELL

MARY MORRISON   BALLANTINE O'SHANTER

CRAIG CAMPBELL   NANNIE O'SHANTER

JENNY CAMPBELL   TAMMY O'SHANTER

DANCERS AND SINGERS, *of the Campbell and O'Shanter Clans*

SETTING: *The open country of Scotland. At center is a rude, plank bridge. At right and left of the bridge are two huge boulders.*

AT RISE: GARTY MACALISTER, *an old man with side whiskers who holds a pipe in his mouth, and* MARY MORRISON, *an old woman with a shawl over her head, are standing leaning on the bridge.*

MARY: And sure with the aches and the miseries, I dinna think I'll live through another horrible, terrible Scotch winter.

GARTY: Aye, sure our winters are the most terrible in creation.

MARY: You speak the truth. After the Almighty made the world, He had nothing left but a rock and a roar, and

179

he threw them down into the North Sea and called them Scotland. I dinna expect to live through another winter. That's the truth.

GARTY: I've been thinking, Mary. Have you ever thought of going to some warm climate for the winter, Mary?

MARY: Sure, I'd never leave Scotland. It would be my death, if I did. That's the truth.

GARTY: Aye, any decent Scot would die of a broken heart away from home. That's the truth. (*Off-stage left, the* CAMPBELLS *sing "Comin' Thro' the Rye."*)

MARY: Aye, listen, Garty. There's a clan a-coming, and they're singing "Comin' Thro' the Rye." It's a bonny song.

GARTY: It's the Campbells. It's the Campbells coming.

MARY: Aye, and don't they sing bonnily.

GARTY: If you don't bridle your tongue, woman, I might as well be listening to the wind. (CAMPBELLS *enter. They stop upstage left of the rock and sing.*)

CAMPBELLS (*Singing*):
>If a body meet a body, comin' thro' the Rye,
>If a body kiss a body, need a body cry?
>Every lassie has her laddie,
>Nane they say, have I,
>Yet all the lads, they smile on me,
>When comin' thro' the Rye.

(*As they finish, they hum and move toward stage center until they are hidden by the rock. They continue humming.*)

MARY: It's a bonny song, "Comin' Thro' the Rye." It fairly sets my feet to dancing. (*The* O'SHANTERS *can now be heard from off-stage right; they are singing the second verse of "Comin' Thro' the Rye."*)

GARTY: Hush your jawing, Mary. I think I hear a second chorus, and it's not coming from the Campbells.

MARY (*Cupping her ear to hear*): I hear it too, Garty. It's the—it's the—

GARTY: Heaven protect us. It's the O'Shanters!

MARY: The Campbells will meet the O'Shanters on this bridge! There will be blood spilled today.

GARTY: And bones broken, too. (*The* O'SHANTERS *enter, stopping right of the rock on the right side of the bridge.*)

O'SHANTERS (*Singing*):
> If a body meet a body, comin' from the well,
> If a body kiss a body, need a body tell?
> Every lassie has her laddie,
> Nane, they say, have I,
> But all the lads they smile on me,
> When comin' thro' the Rye.

(*As they finish, they hum and move toward stage center until they are hidden by the rock. Both the* CAMPBELLS, *behind the rock, left of the bridge, and the* O'SHANTERS *behind rock, right of the bridge, are now humming.*)

MARY: When the Campbells face the O'Shanters on this bridge, there'll be no kissing coming from the well.

GARTY: It will be the kissing of fist and jaw, I'm thinking.

MARY: And it's a pity, too. The Campbells and O'Shanters long were great friends.

GARTY: As close as clan kin, they were.

MARY: And now except for Ellison Campbell and young Tammy O'Shanter, there is nothing but hate between the two clans.

GARTY: And what chance has a wee lassie like Ellison or

a young laddie like Tammy against the hatred of the clans?

MARY: Aye, I'm thinking they're lost, poor wee folk.

GARTY: And it's a pity, too.

MARY: And I'm thinking that an old woman like myself and an old man like you, Garty MacAlister, could be finding a better place to end their days than in the middle of a clan war.

GARTY: Now, just a minute there, Mary. I've got a bit of an idea. Maybe we can end this clan war today.

MARY: And I've an idea you've lost your mind. Sure, didn't even the saintly Brother Sutherland speak to them both, and to no avail.

GARTY: The Reverend spoke to their sense of kindness. I'll speak to their pride.

MARY: I'm thinking it's your last speech you'll be speaking, Garty, if you mix in this feud.

GARTY: I'm thinking it's worth the risk.

MARY: Then be prepared, for they are both coming into view now. (*The singing starts again, from both clans; and the* CAMPBELLS *and the* O'SHANTERS *come into view, headed to meet each other on the bridge.*)

CAMPBELLS *and* O'SHANTERS (*Singing*):
If a body meet a body, coming from the town,
If a body greet a body, need a body frown?
Every lassie has her laddie,
Nane, they say, have I.
But all the lads they smile on me,
When comin' thro' the Rye.

(*Both groups come into view of each other. They walk to either edge of the bridge.* CRAIG *and* JENNY CAMPBELL *continue to the center of the bridge, where they are met by* BALLANTINE *and* NANNIE O'SHANTER. *The clans, except for the leaders, continue to sing, but the closer the leaders get, the softer the singing becomes. When the leaders stand face to face, the singing stops.*)

CRAIG (*To* BALLANTINE): Well, man, are you and your crew going to clear the way to let decent people pass?

BALLANTINE: I was thinking it should be the other way around.

CRAIG: If you don't clear a path, we'll knock you down and walk over you.

BALLANTINE: The Campbell doesn't live who can step high enough to walk over an O'Shanter.

CRAIG: We'll be knocking you so low, it won't take much of a step.

BALLANTINE: If it's a fight you want, that's what you'll get.

CRAIG: That's what I want.

GARTY (*Going between them*): Now, listen, both of you. Is this any way to behave on such a bonny day? To be making such a racket while me and Mary Morrison was quietly enjoying the soft air?

CRAIG: The Campbells have no quarrel with you, Garty. And you heard me offer to let the O'Shanters off free if they would simply remove themselves from our path. Now as a man of some years and sense, Garty, tell me, could I do more?

BALLANTINE: Aye, Garty, as a man of years and sense, tell this big baboon to get his ragged clan out of decent folks' way.

GARTY: Now, you're both asking my opinion.

CRAIG: I'm asking it—

BALLANTINE: And I'll take it, *if* it's the right opinion.

GARTY: As I see it, you're asking me a kind of favor, aren't you both?

CRAIG: You could call it that, I suppose.

BALLANTINE: Though if you convince the Campbells to turn tail and run, it's them that should be that grateful to you.

GARTY: If it's a favor you're asking, it's a favor you should be doing first. That's the Scotch way.

BALLANTINE: Aye, that it is.

CRAIG: Speak on.

GARTY: Now Mary Morrison here and I have been arguing as to which is the greatest dancing clan in Scotland—the Campbells or the O'Shanters. The O'Shanters or the Campbells.

CRAIG: The Campbells, of course.

BALLANTINE: Everyone knows it's the O'Shanters.

GARTY: Aye, that's the trouble. Some say one. Some say the other.

CRAIG *and* BALLANTINE (*Together*): Then some are daft.

GARTY: Aye, that's for sure. But if we could have a dancing contest, we could settle the matter now and for good.

CRAIG: The Campbells will dance the O'Shanters off their feet.

BALLANTINE: The O'Shanters will leave the Campbells panting for breath.

CRAIG: The Campbells are willing. But who's to do the judging?

GARTY: Mary Morrison and I will do the judging.

CRAIG: I suppose that will do. But you'd better judge right.

BALLANTINE: The O'Shanters will take it personal and hard if you don't, old man.

GARTY: If you follow the rules, you'll both be pleased with the judging, I promise you. Now will you go back to your clans and promise to abide by my rules?

CRAIG: I agree, Garty, but I think you may have trouble with the O'Shanters when you give your judgment to us.

BALLANTINE: I agree, too. But I think the Campbells will take it hard when you give the judgment to us. (*The two couples return to their clans, and the clans now move into positions, downstage left and right of the center of the bridge.* GARTY *and* MARY *stand at the rail on the bridge in the center.*)

MARY (*To* GARTY): I hope you know what you're doing, Garty. I always meant to die of a nice, clean Scotch winter, not in the middle of a clan war.

GARTY: Don't go back on me now, Mary. This day will yet end happily. (*Addresses the two clans*) Campbells and O'Shanters. O'Shanters and Campbells. It has been agreed that the question of which is the greatest dancing clan in Scotland shall be settled today with a contest. Everybody knows that it's either the O'Shanters or the Campbells—the Campbells or the O'Shanters. (*Both clans applaud and shout approval.*) But today will see which is the better of the two.

1ST CAMPBELL: It will only be seeing what everybody knows.

2ND CAMPBELL: It will be the Campbells.

1ST O'SHANTER: The Campbells are great shouters, but a little weak on dancing.

2ND O'SHANTER: It will be the O'Shanters.

GARTY: Now, as I am the judge, I will be obeyed. And
we'll have no more yelling until the contest is done.
We'll dance three dances—"The Highland Fling,"
"The Old Hey," and "Miss Falconer's Fancy."

CAMPBELLS: That suits us.

O'SHANTERS: They'll do.

GARTY: Now, since you did not bring your bagpipes with
you, I make this rule. The clan that is not dancing must
do the singing for the clan that is. Agreed?

1ST CAMPBELL: I don't know if we should like to be
singing to the O'Shanters' dancing.

1ST O'SHANTER: And we don't know if we could dance to
the Campbells' singing.

GARTY: The clan that cries "quits" is the loser, of course.

2ND CAMPBELL: Who's crying "quits"? We'll sing.

2ND O'SHANTER: The O'Shanters never quit. We'll dance.

GARTY: Then it's agreed. The Campbells will dance first,
"The Highland Fling." And the O'Shanters will sing
that bonny song, "Loch Lomond." And make it lively,
O'Shanters. It is no funeral march, "The Highland
Fling." (*The* CAMPBELLS *group for the dance, and the*
O'SHANTERS *prepare to sing. There are many variations
of this dance, which may be found in "Dances of Scotland" by Jean C. Milligan and D. G. MacLennan
[Chanticleer Press, 1951]. Any folk dance may be used,
or a dance routine may be improvised. "The Highland
Fling" starts with the couples facing each other. The
heads and shoulders of the dancers are extended slightly
forward and upward, and the hands are at the sides. As
the dance starts, a woman should hold her skirt with
one hand and place the other on her waist. A man places*

*both hands on his own waist. The basic steps are three:
"the round-the-leg," a hopping, skipping step used for
pivoting; the "Highland Schottische," a spring step used
for moving forward, backward, and sideward; and the
"toe-and-heel," used for keeping time. One way of
doing the dance is for one line to start with the "round-
the-leg" while the other does the "toe-and-heel"; then
both do the schottische together. Then they alternate.)*

O'SHANTERS (*Singing*):

By yon bonnie banks and yon bonnie braes,
Where the sun shines bright on Loch Lomond,
Where me and my true love were ever want to gae,
On the bonnie, bonnie banks of Loch Lomond.

Refrain

Oh, ye'll take the high road
And I'll take the low road,
And I'll be in Scotland afore ye;
But me and my true love will never meet again,
On the bonnie, bonnie banks of Loch Lomond.

O'SHANTERS (*Singing*):

'Twas then that we parted in yon shady glen,
On the steep, steep side of Ben Lomond,
Where in purple hue, the Highland hills we view,
And the moon coming out of the gloaming.

(*Refrain is repeated.*)

O'SHANTERS (*Singing*):

The wee birdies sing, and the wild flowers spring,
And in sunshine the waters are sleeping,
But the broken heart it kens nae second spring again,
Tho' the waeful may cease frae their greeting.

(*Refrain is repeated.*)

(*As the dance and the singing end, all are laughing.*)

MARY (*To* GARTY): I'm thinking your plan might work, Garty. They seem less ready for a fight now.

GARTY: Aye, it's hard to keep hatred in your hearts when you're singing and dancing.

MARY: But I'm wondering what will happen when you have to pick the winner. Then the loser will forget the singing and dancing.

GARTY: I don't think they will—if my plan works. (*To the clans*) Now, sure that was a fine dance. And that was fine singing, too. Don't you both agree?

1ST O'SHANTER: The singing was grand. And the dancing wasn't bad for a clan that has nothing but left feet.

1ST CAMPBELL: Aye, the singing *was* grand—for people who don't know one note from another.

GARTY (*Laughing*): Aye, that's the spirit. Good-natured joking shows the stuff we Scots are made of. But let's not stop now. O'Shanters, are you ready to dance "The Old Hey"?

2ND O'SHANTER: Ready to dance it? Why, Garty, we're ready to teach it.

GARTY: And how about all of you Campbells, are you ready to sing? Let's make it that grand old song, "Annie Laurie." And make it lively. (*The* CAMPBELLS *start humming while the* O'SHANTERS *form for "The Old Hey." This is a country dance in which the couples form in a circle. The basic step is the "Highland Schottische." One routine is as follows: the couples form in a circle and come together, then move out; one couple breaks away from the circle, and the others form a bridge by holding their hands together, and the couple dances under it. When the solo couple reaches the end of the bridge, the man and the woman join it; and the next couple dances through. When all the couples have made the trip "under the bridge," the dancers return to the circle formation. The dance is a reel; any reel may be used.)*

CAMPBELLS (*Singing*):

> Maxwellton braes are bonnie,
> Where early fa's the dew,
> And 'twas there that Annie Laurie
> Gave me her promise true;
> Gave me her promise true,
> Which ne'er forgot will be;

Refrain:

> And for Bonnie Annie Laurie,
> I'd lay me doon and dee.

> Her brow is like the snowdrift,
> Her neck is like the swan;
> Her face it is the fairest
> That e'er the sun shone on;
> That e'er the sun shone on,
> And dark blue is her eye,

Refrain:

> And for Bonnie Annie Laurie,
> I'd lay me doon and dee.

(*When the singing and dancing end, all hum the song.*)

GARTY: Another good dance and another fine song! (*The two clan leaders march up, left and right of* GARTY, *and stand looking half at him and half at each other. The humming stops.*) Aye, now that was a bonny dance.

CRAIG: Not so good as the first one. The Campbells dance the better. But it was a good song.

BALLANTINE: Not as good as the first one. The O'Shanters both sing and dance better.

CRAIG: That's a mean judgment. Tell this old bag of wind, Garty, that your judgment is that the Campbells are both the best singers and the best dancers.

BALLANTINE: Aye, Garty, do your judging. And be fair, man, or you'll never judge again.

1ST CAMPBELL (*To other* CAMPBELLS): I shouldn't like to be in Garty's shoes if he judges for the O'Shanters.

2ND CAMPBELL: Nor if he judges for us. For to give the O'Shanters their due, they are terrible fighters.

1ST O'SHANTER (*To other* O'SHANTERS): Poor old Garty has got himself in a fix.

2ND O'SHANTER: Sure, he'll never please both us and the Campbells.

3RD O'SHANTER: Sure, I feel sorry for him.

GARTY: Now, listen to me, all of you. This is breaking the rules. You want a judgment before the contest is over.

CRAIG: You've heard us both sing.

BALLANTINE: And you've seen us both dance.

GARTY: Aye, but there's one more dance—"Miss Falconer's Fancy."

BALLANTINE: It's fine with us. We'll dance it.

CRAIG: Not today you won't. The Campbells will dance it.

BALLANTINE: It's no fair contest if the Campbells dance two and the O'Shanters only one.

GARTY: Aye, that's true. We'll have to do this a new way. Ballantine O'Shanter, who is the best dancer in your clan?

BALLANTINE: It's my own son, Tammy. He's the one.

GARTY: Aye, that's what I've heard. Step out, Tammy.

(TAMMY *steps out from his clan and walks to the middle of the stage.*) And now, Craig Campbell, who is the finest dancer in your clan?

CRAIG: It's my own daughter, Ellison. Everybody knows it.

GARTY: Aye, that's what I've heard. Step out, Ellison. (ELLISON *walks down and stands facing* TAMMY.) Now then, we're ready to begin. Clans of Campbell and O'Shanter, will you provide the music with your own fair voices? Let's all sing, "My Heart's in the Highlands."

CRAIG: Aye, what's this! A Campbell dance with an O'Shanter?

ELLISON: Oh, I'm willing, Father. For the good of the clan, of course. I wouldn't want it to be said my heart wasn't in the Highlands.

TAMMY: And I, too, Father. No O'Shanter ever quits, you know.

GARTY: Then, that's settled. Let the singing begin and the dancing follow.

BALLANTINE (*Folding his arms and looking grim*): I don't approve. But I'll watch it.

CRAIG (*Standing next to* BALLANTINE *in the same pose*): Neither do I, but I'll watch it with you.

BALLANTINE: It's a disgrace. But don't they make a fine couple?

CRAIG: It is indeed a disgrace, but they do indeed look fine.

GARTY (*Shouting to the clans*): Let's start singing then, "My Heart's in the Highlands." (*The clans start singing, first the* CAMPBELLS *and then the* O'SHANTERS *and they join together in the chorus. As they sing,* TAMMY

and ELLISON *dance "Miss Falconer's Fancy." The dance*
starts with a bow; TAMMY *has his hands at his side and*
ELLISON *holds her skirt. The basic step is a ballet step,*
the Pas de Basque, which is followed by two skip-
change-of-steps; then they take an allemande position,
ELLISON *on the left and just in front of* TAMMY. *He*
holds her left hand down with his left hand just in
front of him and her right hand up with his right hand
in back of her. In this position they do eight skipping-
hop steps, and then they join hands for a ring-around
step. At the conclusion of the dance, they step back and
bow to each other.)

CAMPBELLS (*Singing*):

> My heart's in the Highlands,
> My heart is not here;
> My heart's in the Highlands,
> A-chasing a deer.

O'SHANTERS:

> A-chasing a wild deer,
> And following the roe,
> My heart's in the Highlands,
> Wherever I go.

CAMPBELLS:

> When I was in the Highlands,
> It was my use,
> To wear a blue bonnet,
> The plaid and the trews.

O'SHANTERS:

> And now that I've left
> That fair Scottish shore.
> Farewell to Valenderrv
> And bonny Portmore

BOTH (*Chorus*):

>My heart's in the Highlands
>My heart is not here.
>My heart's in the Highlands
>A-chasing a deer,
>A-chasing a wild deer,
>And following the roe.
>My heart's in the Highlands
>Wherever I go.

(*When the song and dance end, there is silence.*)

GARTY (*Trying to start applause*): Now, wasn't that well done? How about some cheers for our dancers?

BALLANTINE: We've had enough of your trickery, Garty. We want a judgment now.

CRAIG: Aye, and it had better be the right one.

GARTY: Well, now. When I heard the O'Shanters sing that bonny song, "Loch Lomond" and saw the Campbells dance "The Highland Fling," I said to myself, "Nothing can be better."

CRAIG: I don't like what you're saying about the singing, Garty.

BALLANTINE: Nor I about the dancing.

GARTY: Will you let me finish! But when I heard the Campbells sing of "Annie Laurie" and watched the O'Shanters dance "The Old Hey," I didn't know what to say.

BALLANTINE: Well, you'd better know now.

GARTY: But then when I saw young Tammy O'Shanter take Ellison Campbell's hand and lead her through "Miss Falconer's Fancy," I knew my winner. The Campbells are great singers and dancers, and so be the O'Shanters, too. But you both are best when joined together to sing and dance on a fair Scotch heath and blend the harmony of your sweet voices with the warmth of your young hearts. Your hearts are in these Highlands, too, and they've got to beat together. That's my judgment now, and I'll stand by it.

MARY: And I'll stand with you, Garty.

BALLANTINE: Aye, and I'm with you, too. (*Offers his hand to* CRAIG) I'm offering you my hand, Craig Campbell.

CRAIG (*Taking his hand*): And I'm taking it, but only for the sake of singing and dancing. Yet my heart's with it, too.

GARTY: Well, now, then there's nothing left to do, but begin the song anew. Scots, let's sing. (*They all sing "My Heart's in the Highlands," as the curtain falls.*)

THE END

THE MAGIC OF SALAMANCA

(Spain)

Author's Notes on THE MAGIC OF SALAMANCA

The sixteenth and early seventeenth centuries were the great years for Spain, her "Golden Age." All Americans know, of course, that it was during this period that Spain opened the New World, and that for much of this time Spain was the leading military nation of Europe. It was also in this period that Spain produced its greatest writers: Lope de Vega, Calderon, and Miguel de Cervantes Saavedra, the author of *Don Quixote*.

Cervantes was not as successful on the stage as he was in his narrative of *Don Quixote;* but he was, nevertheless, influential in helping Spain achieve theatrical glory. Using the theatrical practices of the popular Italian comedy, the *commedia dell' arte,* he made it peculiarly Spanish by blending into that realistic comedy, the Spanish folk beliefs in magic and devils. This play is based on *The Cave of Salamanca,* written and produced by Cervantes about 1600.

The Magic of Salamanca

Characters

PANCRACIO, *the master*
LEONARDA, *the maid*
CARLOS, *the gardener*
PANCHO, *a student from Salamanca*
NICHOLAS, *the butcher's boy*
MARIA, *the baker's girl*

TIME: *About 1600.*
SETTING: *A road.*
AT RISE: PANCRACIO, *carrying a bag, is standing down-stage talking to his two servants,* LEONARDA *and* CARLOS, *both of whom are pretending to weep.*

PANCRACIO: Come, come, my loyal, faithful servants, do not weep. I shall be gone but four days. A mere four days, only ninety-six hours.

LEONARDA: Ninety-six hours! Boo hoo! Each hour will seem like a year.

CARLOS: And ninety-six hours makes . . . let me see (*Counts on his fingers*) five thousand, seven hundred and sixty minutes.

LEONARDA: Boo hoo! Five thousand, seven hundred and

sixty minutes. And each minute will seem like a century.

CARLOS: Five thousand, seven hundred and sixty minutes make . . . let me see (*Counts on fingers again*) three hundred and forty-five thousand, six hundred seconds.

LEONARDA: Boo hoo! Three hundred and forty-five thousand, six hundred seconds, and each second will seem like a thousand years.

PANCRACIO: It is amazing that I am so loved by my servants, but what am I to do if I am such a lovable master? I must go to Madrid to see my only sister entered into solemn matrimony.

LEONARDA: Master Pancracio, we shall miss you terribly until you return. Won't we, Carlos?

CARLOS: Indeed, we shall. I shall not sleep a wink until you return.

LEONARDA: I shall not eat a bite.

PANCRACIO: This is too much. I have made up my mind. I will not go.

CALOS (*Quickly*): Oh, no, master, you must go. What will your sister's neighbors think if you are not there?

LEONARDA: They will think she has no family.

PANCRACIO: But a good servant is more precious than jewels, and if you do not eat and sleep while I am gone, you may be sick.

LEONARDA: I shall eat a little. For your sake, master. So now go.

CARLOS: I shall eat a lot.

PANCRACIO: Not too much. Don't overdo it. Food costs money, you know, and a good servant considers his master's wealth as if it were his own.

CARLOS: Oh, I shall, good master, I shall consider everything you own as though it were my own.

LEONARDAS Hurry, master, the coach is waiting that will take you to Madrid.

PANCRACIO: Well, I shall go if you are sure you will be all right in my absence.

LEONARDA: We shall miss you, but we'll be all right.

PANCRACIO: I shall bring you each a present from Madrid. What would you like, Leonarda?

LEONARDA: I should like some fine stockings.

PANCRACIO: Fine stockings! You are talking like a frivolous lady instead of a good servant. I am shocked. I thought I would bring you a new broom.

LEONARDA: A new broom! That is just what I really wanted, but I thought my master would rather buy fine stockings, for I am told that Señor Pancracio has a reputation of being a fine gentleman in Madrid, and I was afraid that if he bought a broom, his friends would think he was only a sweeper at home.

PANCRACIO: I hadn't thought of that. Maybe you are right. I will think about it on the way. Perhaps I will get you fine stockings in Madrid, and then later you can buy a new broom here in the village. And what would you have me bring you, Carlos?

CARLOS: Only that which would help Master Pancracio's reputation as a fine gentleman in Madrid.

PANCRACIO (*Aside to audience*) That was well said. Perhaps too well said . . . I do not know why my servants should be so considerate of me. . . . I am never considerate of them, and to be treated better than one deserves gives one grounds to be suspicious. . . . But perhaps I am a better master than I thought I was. . . . Or perhaps they are greater fools. . . . I shall have to cut their salaries when I return.

CARLOS: You must hurry, master. The coach will leave without you.

LEONARDA (*Points off right*): See, the driver is turning the horses.

PANCRACIO (*Shouts*): Driver! Driver, wait for me. I am going to Madrid to see my sister married. (*Rushes off stage right.*)

CARLOS (*Shouting after him*): Enjoy yourself in Madrid, Master Pancracio. (*Aside to* LEONARDA) I hope they put him in a cage in Madrid and exhibit him as the meanest master that ever lived.

LEONARDA (*Shouting after* PANCRACIO): Have a good journey, master. (*Aside*) I hope you fall and break your neck.

CARLOS: At last, he's gone! He is on the coach.

LEONARDA: At last! Now, we can have a little fun.

CARLOS: I was afraid there for a moment that he would change his mind and stay. You always overdo things, Leonarda, telling him you would not eat a bite in his absence. Imagine!

LEONARDA: What about yourself, telling him you would not sleep a wink!

CARLOS: And indeed I won't. I can sleep when he returns.

LEONARDA (*Laughs*): What a rascal you are, Carlos!

CARLOS: What a rascal *I* am! And you talking the old goat into bringing you back fine stockings. I wonder what he shall bring me. Perhaps a new fine hat, with a gay feather in it.

LEONARDA: Come, let's not waste time. Our master has

already been gone five minutes, and we have not yet begun to have fun.

CARLOS: Five minutes! That's three hundred seconds!

LEONARDA: Three hundred seconds gone already! How time does fly when Señor Pancracio is away. Let us hurry. Nicholas and Maria will be here soon. I told them to come as soon as they saw the coach leave.

CARLOS: I hope they do not forget the food.

LEONARDA: There is no chance of that. I did not invite the butcher's boy and the baker's girl for nothing. But I wish. . . . (*She stops and pauses.*)

CARLOS: You wish what?

LEONARDA: I wish that someone was coming who would bring music.

CARLOS: I don't! I eat as well in silence as in noise, and he who opens his mouth to sing will later want to open it to eat.

LEONARDA: You have no soul, Carlos, you care nothing for music.

CARLOS: True, but I have a big stomach, and it is crying for food. Let us go into the house and get all the things that we have hidden away for our feast. (*They exit into the house, and* PANCHO *comes along and stops in front of the house. A guitar hangs from a strap around his neck.*)

PANCHO: I have come eighteen miles today, and my feet are screaming and my stomach is pleading with me. "Please, Pancho," it says, "I know you are a wise student, but think no more about great matters and set your mind to ways and means of getting me some food." It is very difficult to be a wise student and think about the heavens and the seas, and things beyond the seas when all the time your stomach is calling, "Get me some food." Perhaps if I play and sing, the birds will come and bring me eggs to eat. It is said all things in nature love music. I will try. (*He takes his guitar, strums a chord and starts to sing "Vagabond Song"* * *or any other Spanish folk song.*

LEONARDA (*Sticking her head out the window*): Troubador, you sing well.

PANCHO: Beautiful Señorita, I sing from hunger, I am no troubador. I am a student from Salamanca.

CARLOS (*Opening the door*): From Salamanca? From the land of the famous caves where devils walk and talk with men and every man is a magician?

LEONARDA: Devils and magic! Who cares for such nonsense? He is a troubador and will sing beautiful love songs.

CARLOS: Love songs! What nonsense when we have a man who can tell us great tales of devils and magic.

LEONARDA: Music!

CARLOS: Magic!

LEONARDA: Music, you ox!

CARLOS: Magic, you magpie!

PANCHO: Wait a minute, my friends. I shall give you both music and magic. But first you must give me something to eat. I have not eaten since early this morning, and surely if I do not eat soon, I shall die.

LEONARDA: Well . . . we are waiting for some friends.

PANCHO: A true friend would not keep you waiting. Let us eat without them.

CARLOS: They are bringing the food.

* #57 in *Singing America*, published by C. C. Birchard, Boston.

PANCHO: We will wait.

LEONARDA: But they will not give you any of their food.

CARLOS: Indeed not, for Nicholas cares for nothing but food.

LEONARDA: And Maria hates music and magic.

CARLOS: But we will ask them.

LEONARDA (*Looking off right*): Here they come now. (*Calls*) Greetings, Nicholas and Maria. Do you bring the food? (NICHOLAS *and* MARIA *enter carrying a huge laundry basket between them. It is covered with a white cloth.*)

NICHOLAS: We have it here. A few little things!

MARIA: A snack really. Just enough to keep us from starving.

NICHOLAS: Some broiled chicken and roast goose . . .

MARIA: Some tender goat and beef . . .

NICHOLAS: A little fish, a few quail . . .

MARIA: Really, just a mouthful of meat . . .

NICHOLAS: A few pieces of fruit: some melon, some grapes . . .

MARIA: A few peaches and pomegranates. . . .

NICHOLAS: Nothing really. Just a mouthful to whet our appetites.

MARIA: Some bread, some pies . . .

NICHOLAS: A few cakes . . .

MARIA: Nothing really. Just a bite to help us stop the horrible pangs of a rather well-developed appetite.

PANCHO: So much food for so few. Oh, how fortunate it is that I stopped here!

MARIA: Who are you?

PANCHO: A hungry student in distress, lovely Señorita.

MARIA: And you'll stay hungry for all of me. I don't intend to go to bed with an empty stomach for the likes of you.

NICHOLAS: Indeed not, and if Leonarda and Carlos have invited you to dine, we'll find another place to eat our lunch.

CARLOS: Oh, indeed not. He was just passing by. Come in. (*He opens the door and stands aside and waves them in. They enter and he turns to* PANCHO.) I'm sorry, my friend, but I'll see what I can do. Stay out here, and I'll sneak some food out to you. But you must show me some magic later.

PANCHO: Thank you, my friend. You do your best, and I shall do mine. (CARLOS *goes into the house and closes the door.*) If I really knew any magic, I would turn those two into the roast pigs they are.

LEONARDA (*Still at the window*): Do not go away, Troubador, and I will sneak some food out to you. But then you must do something for me.

PANCHO: Sing, Beautiful Lady?

LEONARDA: Yes, and something more. I have a feeling that something is going to happen. I want you to stay out here, and if someone should come, warn me.

PANCHO: Gladly, kind lady. (LEONARDA *disappears behind the curtain.*)

PANCHO (*To audience*): This is a fine pickle. There they are eating their heads off, and here I am without a blade of grass to chew on. If Carlos and Leonarda do not help me, I shall die of hunger before the night is out.

CARLOS (*Opening the door and handing him a piece of food*): Here. Do not forget to show me some magic later. (*He closes the door again.*)

PANCHO (*Eating*): Carlos is a good fellow. It is too bad
I do not know any magic to show him, but perhaps
if I eat enough to grow fat, I shall grow wondrously
magical as well.

LEONARDA (*Leaning out of the window and handing him
some food*): Here! Do not forget to keep a good watch
and warn me if someone is coming. (*She sticks her head
back in the window.*)

PANCHO: Leonarda is a good girl, and I can keep watch
for her. That requires no talent. (*Looking off right*)
Here comes someone. I shall warn her, and perhaps she
will give me something more to eat. The fellow looks
harmless enough, but it will show her I am on the
job. (*Calls in the window*) Leonarda, someone is coming.

LEONARDA (*Sticking her head out the window*): Where
is he?

PANCHO: Coming up the road. He carries a bag.

LEONARDA: Oh, it is our master! He has returned. (*Calling to others in house*) Everyone out of the house at
once. (*All tumble out of the house. MARIA and NICHO-
LAS have their mouths stuffed and carry the basket
between them. In this scene, they are barely able to
speak because their mouths are full. They nearly fall
down several times when they try to run away because
each has a hold on the basket, and they try to run in
different directions. There is a good deal of confusion
and rush in this scene until PANCRACIO arrives on stage.*)

CARLOS: Quick, run hide. If Señor Pancracio sees you, we
are in trouble.

LEONARDA: No, not that way. He will see you.

NICHOLAS: Where? Where?

MARIA: I'm afraid. He will see us and tell my master.

CARLOS: No, not that way. (*Grabs them and steers them to the bin*) Quick, hide in the bin. You can leave when he goes in the house.

LEONARDA: Hurry! Hurry! He will catch you. (NICHOLAS *and* MARIA *crawl into the bin, dragging basket after them.*)

CARLOS (*To* PANCHO) Now you, my friend. Quickly.

PANCHO (*Calmly sitting down next to the bin*): Not I. I have done nothing to hide for.

LEONARDA: But, if Señor Pancracio sees you . . .

PANCHO: I am not going to share that sty with those two great porkers.

CARLOS: Come, my friend, just for a little time.

PANCHO: No.

LEONARDA: Come, we haven't got time to argue with him. We must be in the house when Señor Pancracio returns so that he will not look about out here.

CARLOS: Yes, and we must see that everything is in order in the house. (*They exit into the house and close the door.* PANCHO *sits very quietly.* PANCRACIO *enters, talking to himself. He does not see* PANCHO.)

PANCRACIO: A fine how-do-you-do this is. My carriage broke down, and now I must wait until tomorrow to go to Madrid to see my sister married. But there is some good in the worst of things. My servants will be so happy to see me back so soon. Their hearts were breaking to see me leave. (*Calls aloud*) Carlos! Leonarda! Open the door. I am home.

CARLOS (*From inside*): Who's there?

PANCRACIO: It is I, Señor Pancracio, your master.

LEONARDA: It cannot be. Our master is in Madrid.

PANCRACIO: No, no. I am here.

CARLOS: Then who is in Madrid?

PANCRACIO: How should I know who is in Madrid?

CARLOS: Our master would know. He is a fine gentleman in Madrid.

LEONARDA: Our master knows many fine people in Madrid.

CARLOS: Many fine people who can say *don* and *doña*.

LEONARDA: His sister is marrying a man in Madrid.

PANCRACIO: Of course, I know all that.

CARLOS: Then why did you say you did not know who was in Madrid? Why are you lying to us?

LEONARDA: Our master would never lie. He is the finest man that ever lived.

PANCRACIO (*Aside to audience*): Oh, how my servants worship me. (*Turning toward door*) Come, come, open the door and you can see if I am your master or not.

CARLOS: Perhaps our master died, and you are his ghost.

PANCRACIO: That is ridiculous. I never died. Not even once. Maybe I will never die, never.

LEONARDA: How do you know you are not dead now?

PANCRACIO: I . . . I just know, that's all.

CARLOS: Pinch yourself to be sure.

PANCRACIO (*Aside*): Perhaps I am dead, who knows? I will pinch myself to be sure. Wouldn't it be a terrible thing to be dead and not even know it. (*He pinches himself.*) Ouch! Open the door, you idiots. I am alive, and I will beat you if you do not open the door.

CARLOS: It is our master, and he is alive.

LEONARDA: All the good saints be blessed. (*They open the door.*)

CARLOS: Come in, good master, your faithful servants welcome you.

PANCHO (*Standing up*): Good evening, Señor Pancracio.

PANCRACIO (*Startled*): Good gracious, who are you?

PANCHO: I am a poor student, a wanderer by the wayside, hungry and tired.

LEONARDA: He is a troubador, master. I told him to go away.

CARLOS: He is a magician from the Caves of Salamanca, master.

PANCRACIO: A magician from the Caves of Salamanca? I shouldn't like that. It is in the Caves of Salamanca that the devils dwell.

PANCHO: We in Salamanca know how to handle those fellows. We snap our fingers and they come to do our bidding.

PANCRACIO: They do? I should like to see that.

PANCHO: Shall I snap my fingers?

PANCRACIO: No, no, you'd better not. I am sure I should die if I were ever to see an ugly devil in the flesh.

PANCHO: I could have them come in another guise.

PANCRACIO: You could? You could?

PANCHO: Indeed I could. I could even have them come bearing gifts—meat and fruits and bread.

PANCRACIO (*Clapping his hands*): That would be wonderful indeed. But you're sure they wouldn't come looking like ugly devils?

PANCHO: I'll tell you what I'll do, Señor Pancracio. I'll have them come looking like your own townspeople —say the baker's girl and the butcher's boy.

PANCRACIO: They are almost as ugly as devils, but I am not afraid of them. Do it!

PANCHO (*Going to bin and snapping his fingers*): Devils, devils, deep in the earth, come up now in the appearance of the baker's girl and the butcher's boy. And bring food with you.

PANCRACIO: Oh, oh, I hear a noise. (MARIA *and* NICHOLAS *come crawling out, pushing the basket of food before them.*)

PANCHO: Now, Devils, chase the wind until you find yourself again in the Caves of Salamanca. Go! (MARIA *and* NICHOLAS *run off right.*)

PANCRACIO: My goodness. You are some magician all right. I never would have believed it if I hadn't seen it with my own eyes. (*Picking up the basket of food*) But now, you must come and eat, if this devilish food is safe for goodly folk like us.

PANCHO: It's good, have no fear.

CARLOS (*Helping* PANCRACIO *carry the basket into the house*): Señor Pancho, you are certainly the most remarkable magician I ever did see. (CARLOS *and* PANCRACIO *enter house.*)

LEONARDA (*Taking his arm*): If you prove half so fine a troubador, all of Spain will be singing your songs.

PANCHO: I shall try. (*Starts singing "Vagabond Song" or any other Spanish folk song.* LEONARDA *joins him in the song, and the curtain falls.*)

THE END

THE SON OF WILLIAM TELL
(Switzerland)

Author's Note on THE SON OF WILLIAM TELL

This play, *The Son of William Tell,* is based on history, legend, and drama. The event the play commemorates is to the Swiss what July 4, 1776, is to Americans, for in 1307 the Swiss did revolt against the rule of the Austrians and did win the right to self-government. The hero, William Tell, however, is a creature of legend. It was not until 1477, almost two hundred years after the Swiss' successful revolution, that William Tell's exploits first came into being. In that year an unknown poet wrote "The Song of the Origin of the Confederation" and credited William Tell with being the "Liberator of Switzerland."

So well did this creation fit the Swiss temperament, however, that the legend of William Tell became accepted as history, and it was generally believed that William Tell, the brave Swiss archer, was an actual person. In 1853, an historian, Joseph Eutych Kopp, re-studied Swiss documents and showed that Tell was legend, not history. At first this discovery came as a shock to the Swiss, but soon they loved their hero even better because as a legendary figure he would always remain free from re-interpretation, always a hero.

The Son of William Tell

Characters

WILLIAM TELL
WILLIAM ⎫ *Tell's sons*
WALTER ⎭
HEDWIG, *Tell's wife*
GESSLER, *the governor*
FRIESSHARDT, *his lieutenant*
KONRAD ⎫
WERNER ⎬ *mountaineers*
ULRICH ⎭
HILDEGARDE ⎫ *young girls*
ELSBETH ⎭

TIME: *The year 1307, during the Swiss fight for independence from Austria.*

SETTING: *An open meadow near the Swiss Alps, in the Canton of Uri, in Switzerland.*

AT RISE: WALTER *and* WILLIAM *are on stage.* WILLIAM *has a bow and arrow and he is showing* WALTER *how to use them.* WALTER *sits on a rock, trying to pay attention. Note: Only rubber-tipped arrows should be used throughout.*

WILLIAM (*Demonstrating with the bow and arrow*): Then, you draw the arrow slowly back, holding the arm firm. You must never take your eye off the target. (*He stops and looks at* WALTER, *and lets the bow drop down.*) Walter, unless you pay attention, you will never learn to shoot an arrow straight.

WALTER: I cannot even see the target, William. How can I ever hit it?

WILLIAM: If you would be like Father, you must practice, practice, practice. And then practice some more.

WALTER: I could never be like Father if I practiced a million years. I am too small.

WILLIAM (*Going over to him*): Oh, you will grow, my little brother. You will grow, never fear.

WALTER: Two years ago you told me that I should be bigger than you in two years. I am still smaller.

WILLIAM (*Laughing*): But, Little Brother, you *are* bigger than I was when I said it.

WALTER: But I am not bigger than you are now. No, William, I shall always be *little* brother. Even if I should grow as big as our mighty Alps, everyone else would grow twice as big. Then I should feel twice as small. I might as well realize that I will never be anything very much, ever.

WILLIAM: Come, come. Is that the way for a son of William Tell to talk? All the mountains ring with words about our father, and even the Austrian Emperor knows of him and wishes Father were his friend.

WALTER: You may tell me how to shoot an arrow, William, but you need not tell me about Father. I, too, am his son, although only a little one.

WILLIAM: I did not mean to make you angry, Walter.

I just wanted you to remember that you are the son of William Tell.

WALTER: When I was alone on the mountainside and the hungry, wild dogs were closing in on me, did not my father find me and shoot the dogs? Father saved my life. I will not forget I am his son.

WILLIAM: I am sorry I said anything, Walter.

WALTER: And who made my bow for me? Answer me that.

WILLIAM: I know, Walter. I said I was sorry. I have no right to tell you how a son of William Tell should behave.

WALTER: Yet, you are right. I am not tall or brave, nor do I shoot straight with an arrow. I am not a very good son of William Tell.

WILLIAM (*Laughing*): You are a funny fellow, Walter. One minute you are ready to fight me for reminding you that you are the son of William Tell and the next minute you say things about yourself that even Gessler, the Emperor's governor, would not say.

WALTER: Gessler! How I hate that name!

WILLIAM: Hush, little brother, you must not say that. He is the governor here, whether we like it or not.

WALTER: By what right does the German tyrant, Albrecht, send Gessler to govern over us?

WILLIAM: Little brother, not so loud. Albrecht is mighty and we Swiss are few.

WALTER: I am not afraid of Albrecht.

WILLIAM: Remember what Father has said. We must do nothing to offend Gessler.

WALTER: I do not see why not. He offends us by being here.

WILLIAM: If we can live with him as governor, we *will*

live with him. That is what Father says. War is a terrible thing, Walter.

WALTER: Slavery is worse.

WILLIAM: What is this talk of slavery? Are we not free to come and go as we please?

WALTER: So long as we bare our heads to the governor. It is not freedom when a Swiss must bow down to the conqueror.

WILLIAM: It is a little thing to take off one's hat.

WALTER: Freedom is also a little thing—to Gessler.

WILLIAM: Well, speak no more about it, now. Here comes Gessler with his lieutenant, Friesshardt.

WALTER: Look how they walk! Like peacocks. They act as if they owned the earth.

WILLIAM: Hush, little brother. (GESSLER *and* FRIESSHARDT *enter, swaggering.* WILLIAM *removes his hat.*)

GESSLER: Well, what do we have here? Two mountain boys. One with manners and one without.

FRIESSHARDT (*Taking* WALTER's *hat from his head and throwing it on the ground*): That means you, boy. Hasn't your father taught you to show respect for your superiors?

WALTER: My father teaches me all things that a boy should know. He is William Tell.

GESSLER: Oh, Tell's son, are you? I should have guessed by your bad manners. Well, pick up your hat, boy. (WALTER *does not move, and* WILLIAM *hastily picks the hat up for him.*) I told *him* to pick it up, boy.

WILLIAM: I am his brother, sir, and I thought I could do it for him.

GESSLER: *Sir?* Evidently you are better instructed than your brother.

FRIESSHARDT: Perhaps he is a little out of his head, Governor. He doesn't look quite right to me.

WILLIAM: He is very bright, sir. It is just that he is young.

WALTER: Too young to bow down to a tyrant.

GESSLER: Oh ho, the little mouse is a rebel.

FRIESSHARDT: Perhaps the little mouse needs to learn what happens to rebels.

HEDWIG (*Off-stage, calling*): William! Walter! Where are you?

GESSLER: Who is that?

WILLIAM: It is our mother, sir. She calls us to come to the meal. (*Shouts*) We are coming, Mother.

GESSLER: Wait a minute. You do not go so easily.

FRIESSHARDT: Indeed not. You have insulted the governor and the crown.

WILLIAM: He meant no harm, sir. Surely, a small boy cannot be expected to—

FRIESSHARDT: No boy is small enough to be beneath the notice of the Emperor.

GESSLER: It is not the small boy I was referring to. It is you, boy. You shouted in my presence. That is an insult. (*Enter* HEDWIG.)

HEDWIG: Walter, William! Why did you not come when I called you?

GESSLER: They did not come, woman, because I told them to stay.

HEDWIG: Sir?

FRIESSHARDT: They were impudent, woman.

HEDWIG: My sons impudent? I cannot believe it.

FRIESSHARDT: Do you call us liars, woman?

HEDWIG: I do not call you anything.

GESSLER: Do you know who we are?

HEDWIG: I know.

GESSLER: I am Gessler, governor by the royal order of his majesty, Albrecht.

HEDWIG: And I, Governor, am the daughter of Walter Furst and the wife of William Tell.

GESSLER: These petty local connections do not impress me.

HEDWIG: Good. Then you will not object if we petty persons take our leave. Our petty supper is waiting.

FRIESSHARDT (*Grabbing her arm*): Wait, woman. You cannot speak to the governor in this fashion.

HEDWIG (*Looking at him without fear*): You must be a brave man, Lieutenant, to lay hands on the wife of William Tell. (FRIESSHARDT *drops his hand quickly*.)

GESSLER: Has your husband not told you we are to be obeyed?

HEDWIG: He has told me that you are the law and as such you are to be respected.

GESSLER: And do you call this respect?

HEDWIG: I do not call bothering children and women the law. And if you are not the law, then I do not respect you.

GESSLER: You do not agree with your husband that it is better to submit?

HEDWIG: Whatever my husband says has my agreement. Law is better than disorder, and peace is better than war.

GESSLER: You do not act as though you agree.

HEDWIG: When you threaten my children, you give me no chance to agree.

GESSLER: Woman, I am not afraid of either your father

or your husband. William Tell means nothing to me.

HEDWIG (*Looking offstage*): Then you may tell him yourself, for here he comes. (*Enter* WILLIAM TELL, *followed by the mountaineers,* KONRAD, WERNER, *and* ULRICH, *and by the little girls,* HILDEGARDE *and* ELSBETH. *They are talking and excited.*)

KONRAD: Hedwig, you should have seen your husband.

WERNER: Two hundred feet if it were an inch, and his arrow cut cleanly.

ULRICH: As if he merely pushed it through.

HILDEGARDE: Oh, Walter, it was so exciting. The great bird was flying after Elsbeth, and your father shot it.

ELSBETH: It would surely have caught me and carried me off if it hadn't been for your father. (WILLIAM *joins mountaineers and girls, who withdraw slightly, talking and laughing.* GESSLER *approaches* TELL.)

GESSLER: It appears you are a hero, Tell.

TELL: Your Excellency flatters me.

GESSLER: No indeed, I don't. The mountains ring with praise of your exploits with the bow and arrow. Isn't that true, Friesshardt?

FRIESSHARDT: Whatever the governor says is always true.

GESSLER: Do you hear that, Tell? Friesshardt agrees.

TELL: Then I am pleased that the governor is pleased.

GESSLER: Perhaps you would give me an example of your skill.

TELL: It is a mean skill at best, your Excellency.

GESSLER: You are much too modest, Tell. I insist.

TELL: Then, of course, I shall be glad to do as you say.

GESSLER (*Taking an apple out of the hands of* HILDEGARDE): Could you hit a target this size?

TELL: If the distance were not too great, I might.

GESSLER: Werner, how far away did you say Tell was when he shot the great bird?

WERNER: About a hundred feet, your Excellency.

FRIESSHARDT: He said two hundred, Governor.

GESSLER: Let's split the difference. We'll make it one hundred and fifty feet. Does that seem fair to you, Tell?

TELL: I can try, your Excellency.

GESSLER: But can you hit it, Tell?

TELL: Perhaps. If my arm is steady and my aim is true.

GESSLER: But let's make it a real contest. (*Gives apple to* WALTER) Here, boy, you set the apple on the target. Walk one hundred and fifty feet in that direction (*Motions toward stage left*), and set the target up.

WALTER: Where shall I set it? By that tree?

GESSLER: No, boy. On your head, where you like to keep your hat.

TELL: You can't mean it!

GESSLER: But I do. What is the danger when the archer is the mighty William Tell?

TELL: I refuse. I won't risk my son's life.

GESSLER: Then Friesshardt will do the shooting, and his aim is always a little low. (*Reaches out and touches* WALTER *on the heart*) It should hit just about here.

HEDWIG: You wouldn't dare!

GESSLER: But I do dare. You peasants need a lesson. You need to learn right at the start who gives commands and who obeys. Draw your sword, Friesshardt, and serve as honor guard here for our young target holder. Now march, boy. (FRIESSHARDT *draws his sword and holds it at* WALTER'S *back.*)

TELL: Governor, I beg of you. Do not force me to risk my own son's life. Kill me, if that is what you wish.

WALTER: Do not beg him, Father. I am not afraid. I am the son of William Tell.

GESSLER: See, Tell, your son has faith in you. Right up until the moment of his death. And do not miss, Tell, for if you do, Friesshardt will not. Do you understand me, Lieutenant?

FRIESSHARDT: I understand, Governor. Now march, young rebel, or you shan't live long enough for your father to kill you. (*They march left until they are offstage.*)

TELL: Governor, I warn you, you go too far.

GESSLER: Keep cool, Tell. Your hands will shake if you lose your temper.

HEDWIG: Governor, spare my child. I will bow down to you.

GESSLER: So, woman, now you know I have a title.

WILLIAM: Excellency, do not do this terrible thing.

GESSLER: Quiet, all of you. For too long now, I have heard all your big talk of William Tell. Now we shall see how big and brave he is. (*Yells to* FRIESSHARDT) That is far enough, Lieutenant. Cover the boy's eyes.

FRIESSHARDT (*off*): Yes, Governor.

WALTER (*Off*): I do not need my eyes covered. I am not afraid when my father holds the bow.

GESSLER: He has courage, Tell. That I'll admit. Let's see how long it lasts. Are you ready? (TELL *takes his bow and each of the mountaineers hands him an arrow. He places two arrows in his belt and strings the third.*)

TELL (*Shouts to* WALTER): Are you ready, Walter? Are you ready, my son?

WALTER (*Off*): I am ready, Father. (TELL *raises the bow to shoot.*) But wait, Father.

GESSLER: The little rebel's courage fails him now that the test comes. I knew as much.

TELL: Governor, I—

GESSLER: It seems that the son of William Tell is not above fear, after all.

WALTER (*Shouting from offstage*): I just wanted to ask you, Father—

GESSLER: He still has a good voice, even if he has no heart.

TELL (*Ignoring* GESSLER): Yes, my son?

WALTER: After you split the apple with your arrow, Father, may I have half or must I give it all back to Hildegarde? (*The mountaineers laugh and cheer.*)

HILDEGARDE: You may have the bigger half, Walter.

WALTER: They will both be the same size, Hildegarde. My father is a fair man.

GESSLER: Well, get on with the contest. Let's see if your deeds today match the big words, and if you can shoot as well as your son talks. (TELL *draws back and shoots. The crowd watches the flight of the arrow and then shouts. For safety reasons, Tell may pretend to shoot arrows.*)

HEDWIG: You hit! You hit the apple. Our son is saved!

ULRICH: And the apple is split!

ELSBETH: And it looks to be right in the middle!

WILLIAM: But Friesshardt has not put away his sword. (TELL *puts another arrow in his bow and shoots again.*)

KONRAD: Look! He has hit Friesshardt.

WERNER: Friesshardt has fallen.

TELL: He has fallen as any man will fall who holds a sword over my son's head. Yea, or any son of Switzerland. (*He draws the third arrow from his belt.*) And this is the arrow that I have saved for you, Gessler.

GESSLER: Wait. Wait. For heaven's sake, wait. I did not mean to harm your son.

TELL: Do not crawl, Gessler. I do not mean to kill you— now. But if ever I see you again in the Canton of Uri, my arrow shall find its mark in your heart. Take that message to your master.

WERNER: And take this message with you, too. We Swiss will bow our heads no more. We will be free or we will be dead.

TELL: Now go quickly, Gessler, and go far. I do not wish to be ashamed for attacking an unarmed man. But if you stay, I'll surely kill you.

GESSLER: All right, I'm going. (*Starts off*) But remember this, Tell, whether you kill me or not, the Emperor's men will come.

TELL: We will be ready to meet them.

ULRICH: And if we should die, the Emperor will still find there are thousands to take our places.

GESSLER: You'll regret this. (*He exits.*)

TELL: We may well regret this. But there was no choice.

ULRICH: At least now I feel like a man again. (WALTER *returns onstage with the apple split in two and the arrow.* HEDWIG *goes to him.*)

HEDWIG: You stood straight and calm, Walter. I am proud of you.

WILLIAM: You are truly a son of William Tell now, Walter.

HILDEGARDE: Walter, you may have all my apple. You were so brave.

WALTER: Father, tomorrow I will start practicing with the bow and arrow. To be a Swiss means one needs to be ready at all times. And I will try to be brave.

TELL: My son, today you gave us all a lesson in bravery. And if Switzerland needs only to wait until you are brave, Switzerland is ready now.

ALL: Switzerland is ready. Freedom for Switzerland. Freedom forever. (*They raise their arms high and come together as the curtain falls.*)

THE END

JOHNNY APPLESEED
(United States)

Author's Notes on JOHNNY APPLESEED

Johnny Appleseed is one of America's greatest heroes, not only for what he did—helping to spread American civilization west, but also for what he was: a kindly, saintly man. His life belongs to both history and legend, and this play draws from both sources. Some of the stories told about Johnny have also been told about other American heroes. The saw-horse episode, for example, is also a part of the Lincoln legend. But Johnny's story is not merely the legend of a man; it's also the legend of a nation, for Johnny is a great slice of American history.

Born John Chapman in Massachusetts at the beginning of the Revolutionary War, he spent his life moving west, being a friend to his fellow men, to the animals, to nature itself. Wherever he went, he carried with him his appleseeds, his love, his justice; and wherever he went, there now grow apples and monuments to Johnny Appleseed. When he died, Senator Sam Houston, later the first president of the Republic of Texas, said of him: "This old man was one of the most useful citizens of the world in his humble way . . . and generations yet unborn will rise up and call him blessed." And generations, not only of statesmen, but of poets and authors have.

Whenever Americans have become concerned with the Frontier concept of America—with brotherhood, with kindliness, with service for others—Johnny Appleseed's name has been fitted to their songs and his appearance characterized on their stage. Vachel Lindsay, for example, wrote a number of poems about Johnny; and in 1938, two well-known playwrights, Marc Connelly and Arnold Sungaard, wrote a play about him, called *Everywhere I Roam.*

Johnny Appleseed

Characters

MIKE FOGLE
MYRTLE FOGLE
MR. FOGLE
MRS. FOGLE
GRANDMA FOGLE

JOHNNY APPLESEED
BULLY BOB BYRNE
BIG BILL SLATTERY
DEADEYE DICK WAGNER

SETTING: *A clearing in the wilderness, somewhere in Ohio during the early years of the nineteenth century.*
AT RISE: MIKE *and* MYRTLE, *two frontier children, are stacking logs.*

MIKE: If I ever met Bully Bob and his crew and if I had a gun, I'd just shoot the feathers out of their hats and tell them if I ever saw them around our place again, I'd shoot them dead.

MYRTLE: Wouldn't you be at all afraid, Mike?

MIKE: Golly, no. What's there for me to be afraid of?

MYRTLE: Papa's afraid of them.

MIKE: He is not.

MYRTLE: He says he is.

MIKE: Grown-ups say lots of things. If Papa didn't have to worry about taking care of you and Mama and

Grandma, why, shucks, he'd just chase Bully Bob all the way to the Mississippi River. Us Fogle men just don't scare.

MYRTLE: I don't see why Papa doesn't do it then. It would sure be a lot nicer around here if we didn't have to worry about outlaws.

MIKE: Golly! You can't explain anything to girls.

MYRTLE: I don't see. . . .

MIKE: You don't see! Well, I'll tell you one thing, you'll never see the day when anything scares Pa or me. (*Enter* JOHNNY APPLESEED, *wearing a pair of ragged trousers, a flour sack for a shirt, a saucepan for a hat. He has a bag of appleseeds over his back, and attached to a rope around his waist he has a green pouch in which he has a Bible.*)

MYRTLE (*Pointing past* MIKE *at him*): Look, Mike!

MIKE (*Turning*): What? (*Sees* JOHNNY, *and is frightened*) A bear! (*Grabs a chunk of wood*) Hurry, Myrtle, run for the cabin. I'll try to keep him back.

MYRTLE (*Grabbing his arm to stop him from throwing the wood*): Stop, Mike. It's not a bear. It's a man.

MIKE: So it is. But it's a funny-looking man.

JOHNNY (*Coming toward them*): That's the truth, son, I never said any different. But you can't go around throwing things at people just because they are not pretty.

MYRTLE: Mike doesn't mean any harm, Mister. He was just scared.

MIKE: I was not. I was just surprised.

MYRTLE: You thought he looked like a bear.

JOHNNY: It would have to be a mighty puny bear, I guess.

MYRTLE (*To* MIKE): And you said you weren't afraid of anything!

JOHNNY: Well, little lady, he was going to stand between you and anything that could hurt you, and that doesn't seem much like being afraid to me.

MYRTLE: But . . . (*Stops and realizes*) You're right, Mister. I'm sorry, Mike. I should be saying thank you. You *are* brave.

MIKE: Say, Mister, you're not one of Bully Bob's outlaws, are you?

JOHNNY: No, Mike. My name's John Chapman. Folks call me Johnny!

MYRTLE: Johnny! Johnny Appleseed! That's who you are, isn't it?

JOHNNY: Some folks call me that, and I like the name well enough.

MYRTLE (*Going up and looking at him*): Is that really a pan you're wearing?

JOHNNY: Sure is, honey. It makes a fine hat, and there aren't many hats you can cook your supper in.

MYRTLE: Could I . . . that is, would you let me . . . ?

JOHNNY: Could you try it on? Sure thing. (*He sets it on her head.*) Now, you look like one of those fine ladies going to church in Boston. Maybe Mrs. John Adams herself.

MYRTLE (*To* MIKE.) Do I look like Johnny Appleseed, Mike?

MIKE (*Who has been stunned during this time*): Johnny Appleseed! Are you really Johnny Appleseed?

JOHNNY: I was when I woke up this morning.

MIKE: I've been hearing about you since I was just that

high (*Indicates size with his hand*), but I never thought I'd see you. I heard that you never wear shoes because your feet are tougher than leather. Is that right?

JOHNNY: Sometimes I wear shoes, but most of the places I like to go don't sell shoes. Sometimes my Indian friends give me moccasins to wear though.

MIKE: I hear you've been all the way to the Mississippi and that you've got a wolf for a friend, and even the great bears like you.

MYRTLE: And the birds and little rabbits are your friends, too, aren't they?

MIKE: And you go wherever you like—and no one ever made you go to school, I'll bet.

JOHNNY: (*Sitting down on a log, as* MIKE *and* MYRTLE *sit down beside him. He takes Bible from his sack.*) Well, I tell you, Mike. I didn't used to like school much, but after my Ma taught me to read this book, I've never missed a day of school since.

MIKE: Aw, Johnny, you're just saying that. You don't go to school any more.

JOHNNY: I can't still go to a proper sort of school with books and slates, but I go to school. Why just this morning, I was studying with old Professor Squirrel, and by the way he was storing his nuts, he taught me a real lesson. It's going to be a cold winter, and I'd better see that all my friends are ready for it. Now, that's going to school, isn't it, Mike?

MIKE: I guess so. But not reading and that stuff.

JOHNNY: There's lots of reading to be done, of course. I saw some wheel ruts back over the last hill, and they pointed this way, and it was just like a lesson in a book telling me that I had friends up ahead. That's reading, isn't it, Mike?

MIKE (*With disgust*): I mean book reading.

JOHNNY: That's the best kind of all. Those wheel ruts told me a wagon had passed, but it was this Bible (*Holds up Bible*) that told me I had *friends* waiting. That's what I really wanted to know. This good, old reading Book tells me what I'm supposed to do with my life.

MYRTLE: Did the Book tell you to plant appleseeds, Johnny?

JOHNNY: It sure did, honey.

MIKE: Ma reads to us out of that Book, and I don't recollect anything about appleseeds.

JOHNNY (*Sitting down*): You don't? You remember about the flood, don't you?

MYRTLE: I remember that. Noah built an ark.

JOHNNY: That's right. Old Noah built an ark, and he was saved. Then God came to him and told him to plant seeds and see that the whole world came to life again. And that's just what old Noah did, and that's just what I'm doing.

MIKE: But God didn't say *apple*seeds.

JOHNNY: It just stands to reason, Mike, that if you are going to plant seeds, there's nothing better than appleseeds.

MYRTLE: Do you have some appleseeds for us to plant?

JOHNNY (*Taking seeds from his bag*): I sure do, honey. You take them and run down to that clearing by the stream and plant them.

MYRTLE (*Taking seeds*): Thank you, Johnny, I will. The next time you come visiting, I'll bake you an apple pie and give you a big pitcher of apple cider. (*Returns his hat*) Thank you for letting me wear your hat, Johnny. It's a lovely hat. (*Exit* MYRTLE, *running*)

JOHNNY: Don't you want to plant some appleseeds, too, Mike?

MIKE: I guess so, but it sure takes a long time for an apple tree to grow, and with all this talk, my mouth is watering for some apple pie right now. (*He takes the seeds from* JOHNNY *and runs after* MYRTLE. JOHNNY *settles down to read, and* MR. *and* MRS. FOGLE *and* GRANDMA FOGLE *come out of the house.*)

MRS. FOGLE (*Calling*): Michael—Michael—Michael! Now where can those young-uns have gone? They were here the last time I looked.

GRANDMA: Children are like birds on the wing. *Just here* means *was there* by the time you get the words out.

MR. FOGLE: I told them to stay right in sight of the cabin. There's no telling what could be happening to them with thieving outlaws like Bully Bob and his ugly crew around. I tell you, Faith, we made a mistake coming West. We ought to go back to Philadelphia.

MRS. FOGLE: Now, Nathaniel, stop worrying. They're around.

GRANDMA: Bully Bob and his crew are no worse than those carriages racing through the streets in Philadelphia. Not as bad, I suspect.

JOHNNY (*Rising and going to them*): If you're looking for your young-uns, they're down by the stream planting an apple orchard.

MRS. FOGLE: Bless me! Where did you come from?

GRANDMA: Good heavens, he's wearing a pan for a hat. Must be daft.

MR. FOGLE: Say, mister, don't I know you from some place?

JOHNNY: Maybe so, Mr. Fogle. I've been here, there, and everywhere planting seeds.

MRS. FOGLE: What kind of seeds do you plant?

JOHNNY: Appleseeds, ma'am.

MRS. FOGLE (*Excited*): Why, I know who you are. You're Johnny Appleseed! I just can't believe it. I never thought you really existed.

JOHNNY (*Laughing*): Lots of folks don't—even after they see me, Mrs. Fogle.

MR. FOGLE: How come you know who we are?

JOHNNY: Out here, we're all neighbors, Mr. Fogle—or we should be. I just passed by to see if I could be of any help.

MR. FOGLE: Why thank you, Johnny. Are you still planting your appleseeds?

JOHNNY: Yes, sir. It's good business. I plant them going West and eat apple pie going back East for another load. Why your little girl just promised me apple pie and apple cider when I come back this way again.

MR. FOGLE: You'll be eating it in Philadelphia then. I can't fight this wilderness any longer. I don't mind the work, but with Bully Bob and his crew, I don't see any chance for a man and his family to grow a crop and live.

JOHNNY: Has old Bob been bothering you?

MR. FOGLE: He hasn't yet, but he will. Why he and his boys went over to Franklinville just a few weeks back and shot up the whole town.

JOHNNY: Bob doesn't like towns, and that's a fact.

MRS. FOGLE: There's no sense in worrying about Bully

Bob and his kind. They probably don't even know we're here.

MR. FOGLE: Oh, they know we're here.

JOHNNY: That's a fact. If there's anything going on in these parts, Bully Bob knows about it. But it's a fact, too, that if he meant you any harm, you'd have heard from him by this time.

MRS. FOGLE: You see, Nathaniel? You listen to Johnny Appleseed. He spreads good sense as well as good apples.

GRANDMA: That makes good sense, Nathaniel.

MR. FOGLE: We'll see how much good sense. Here come Bob and his boys now. I'm going back to the house to get my gun.

JOHNNY: I wouldn't do that. If you can see Bob, he can see you, and anything Bob can see, he can hit, too. Just stand firm and we'll see what happens. (*Enter* BULLY BOB BYRNE, BIG BILL SLATTERY, *and* DEADEYE DICK WAGNER.)

BULLY BOB (*In a loud voice*): If it isn't old Johnny Appleseed!

JOHNNY: Hello, Bob. I've been wondering when I would see you. You move a little further West every time I see you, it seems.

BIG BILL: Got to keep moving to get away from civilization. Towns are just spreading faster than a brush fire in a dry season.

DEADEYE DICK: Civilization! It makes me want to shoot every time I hear that word. It's just a fancy word for making a fellow wear tight shoes and a tie.

JOHNNY: I hear you boys were shooting up Franklinville civilization a few weeks back.

BULLY BOB: Shucks, we were just waking them up a little, so they could see what live men look like.

BIG BILL: That's a terrible place over there, Johnny. Saw two fellows working behind a counter in a store and taking orders from a woman! Now is that anything for a *man* to be doing?

DEADEYE DICK: Are these here settlers friends of yours, Johnny?

JOHNNY: Old friends, Dick. In fact, just like brothers.

BULLY BOB: Everybody's just like brothers to you, Johnny.

BIG BILL: Johnny even thinks the wolves are his brothers.

JOHNNY: That's what the Good Book says, you know.

BULLY BOB: Don't you start preaching to us, Johnny. I'm not going to listen to anybody preaching.

BIG BILL: Let him do a little preaching. I like to hear the stories he tells. I never did find out what happened to that fellow in the lions' den.

BULLY BOB: How would you like me to shoot a few holes in your head, Bill?

JOHNNY: Now, now, Bob. Don't be flying off the handle that way.

BULLY BOB: I'll fly off the handle if I want to. They don't call me Bully Bob for nothing.

GRANDMA: I thought they just called you Old Bull.

BULLY BOB: Old Bull!! I'd kill the man who called me that.

JOHNNY: You know, Bob, your bark's a lot worse than your bite.

BULLY BOB (*Roaring*): What did you say?

JOHNNY (*Very calmly*): In fact, Bob, when it comes right down to it, you're a pretty kindly man. Why I remember when you carried that little Sullivan girl right through a blizzard to get her to a doctor.

BULLY BOB: What do you want to talk about things like that for? Do you want to ruin my good name?

JOHNNY: Nobody even thought you'd make it alive.

BULLY BOB: That was different. She was just a little kid. I don't hate kids. I just hate people! Like these settlers here. (*Shouts*) I hate settlers.

JOHNNY: You just like to roar, Bob. Now what did you come visiting for today? Did you come to offer to help my friends here?

BULLY BOB: What! Me help settlers! Why it would be just like cutting my own throat.

DEADEYE DICK: We came to tell them to get out of here. That's what we came for.

BIG BILL: Wherever there's settlers, there's bound to be towns.

DEADEYE DICK: And towns mean civilization—and I sure hate that word.

JOHNNY: Just a minute. You're not thinking right. Towns are going to come whether you like it or not. But these good farm folks aren't going to build the towns. They're the ones that are going to keep the country green and the air pure and sweet. Why right now their young-uns are down by the river planting some of my appleseeds. Does that sound like folks who intend to turn the place into a town?

DEADEYE DICK: Planting appleseeds, eh?

BIG BILL: That means apple pie.

BULLY BOB: Wait one minute there. I might just let the kids stay, but these people have got to go. They're grown-ups—and grown-ups are people.

JOHNNY: I don't rightly think that I can let you run these good folks off, Bob.

BULLY BOB: Now, Johnny, I like you fine, but there's not anybody that's going to stand in Bully Bob's way and live.

JOHNNY: Maybe not, Bob, but I might just have to try.

BULLY BOB: I'd just eat you alive, Johnny, appleseeds and all.

JOHNNY: You might find me a little tough to digest, especially when you got to my feet. I've got awfully tough feet, Bob.

BULLY BOB (*Laughing*): You really would stand up and fight, wouldn't you? I'm twice your size, half your age, and a whole lot meaner; and you'd stand up to me. I've got to say this, Johnny Appleseed. Folks may think you're crazy as a loon, but you have a lot of nerve. I'll tell you what I'll do. We'll have a contest to see who's the stronger. If I am, you step out of the way. If you are, I'll never bother these folks again.

JOHNNY: All right, Bob, but I get to pick the contest. All right?

BULLY BOB: Anything you say: knives, fists, guns. You name it.

JOHNNY: I could say that we could stick pins in our feet and see who hollers first.

BULLY BOB: Oh, now, Johnny, that's not fair. You got feet just like leather, and my feet are tender.

JOHNNY: That's right, Bob. You're a riding man, aren't you?

BULLY BOB: Sure as shootin', I am. I ride the biggest, toughest horse in the West.

JOHNNY: I'll tell you what I'll do then. We both sit on a

horse, and we expect it to carry us. It's only fair we carry the horse.

BULLY BOB: What? How can a man carry a horse? No man can do that.

JOHNNY: I can.

BULLY BOB: You cannot, Johnny. I'll just bet you can't.

JOHNNY: All right, now. If I can carry the last horse I sat on, will you admit that I win the contest?

BULLY BOB: That I'll do, and if you don't, I'm just going to shoot you full of holes for telling such a fool lie.

JOHNNY: You wait here, and I'll carry my horse to you. (JOHNNY *exits*.)

BULLY BOB: I'm going to shoot that old man and enjoy it. He thinks I'm a fool.

GRANDMA: Young man, why are you always shooting people? Do you want to get a bad name?

BULLY BOB: Yes, ma'am. That's what I've been working for all my life, a good bad name. (BIG BILL *and* DEAD-EYE DICK *laugh loudly*.)

BULLY BOB: Quiet down, you two buzzards.

MR. FOGLE: Here comes Johnny—and he's carrying his horse.

JOHNNY (*Entering, carrying a sawhorse*): Here's my horse, Bob, and I'm carrying him.

BULLY BOB: Why, it's nothing but a sawhorse.

JOHNNY (*Setting it down*): Didn't say what kind it was.

GRANDMA: Sure didn't. He didn't say what kind it was, just the last one he sat on.

JOHNNY: And Old Wooden Sides here is the gentlest horse I ever sat on. Doesn't eat much, either.

BULLY BOB: It's a goldarned trick.

JOHNNY: It sure is, Bob, on you. Are you a big enough man to stand by your bargain?

BULLY BOB: I wasn't going to chase them off anyway, but it's just because of their young-uns.

JOHNNY: Mike and Myrtle will be real pleased, Bob, and here they come now. (*Enter* MIKE *and* MYRTLE *running.*)

MIKE: Look Myrtle, it's the outlaws!

MYRTLE: It's Bully Bob.

MIKE: And Deadeye Dick.

MYRTLE: And Big Bill Slattery.

BULLY BOB: They're pretty young, Johnny.

JOHNNY: Nowhere near people-size yet, are they, Bob?

BULLY BOB: I'm kind of glad you found a horse you could carry, Johnny. I'd have hated to shoot you.

MIKE (*To his father*): What have they come for, Pa? Are they going to make us leave?

JOHNNY: Why, shucks, no. They've come over to help your folks, haven't you, Bob?

BULLY BOB: I guess so. (*Quickly*) But there's nothing much we can do.

DEADEYE DICK: Because we don't know much about farm work.

BIG BILL: And we're not fixing to learn.

JOHNNY: What they really came for, Mike, was to give your folks a horse. An oat-eating one. Isn't that right, Bob?

MYRTLE: Well, you certainly are a sweet man, Mr. Bob.

BULLY BOB: I suppose so. (*To* DICK) Dick, you take your horse around back and put it in the barn. You can ride back to camp with me—unless you want to ride

Johnny's horse. Haw. Haw. Then we'd better get out of here while we still got our guns and two horses left. Doggone it, Johnny, when it comes to ruining a man, there's nothing worse than a good man, a small girl, and a wooden horse. Let's go, men.

MRS. FOGLE: I just don't know how we'll ever thank you, Mr. Bob.

BULLY BOB: No need to thank us. Just don't start any town here.

DEADEYE DICK: 'Cause if you do, we'll come back and shoot it up.

MIKE: I'd bet that would be something to see. (*Exit* BOB, BILL, *and* DICK.)

MR. FOGLE: I don't know how I'm ever going to thank you, Johnny. It was just a miracle, that's what it was.

JOHNNY: Maybe so. But it's not my miracle. It's just plumb impossible for a man to be all bad in a country like this.

GRANDMA: That Bully fellow is sure trying.

JOHNNY: He sure is, Grandma Fogle, and maybe that's one of the best tests that we got the right kind of country. If a country is only as good as its good people, it's got a rough road ahead. But when a country's so good that even the bad ones turn out to be heroes every once in a while, that's a country with the right idea.

GRANDMA: I'll say amen to that, Johnny.

ALL: Amen! (*Curtain*)

THE END

PRODUCTION NOTES

Production Notes

The Double Nine of Chih Yuan

Characters: 3 male; 2 female.

Playing Time: 15-20 minutes.

Costumes: Chinese pajama-type costumes in various colors.

Properties: Stepladder, toy turtle, doll, kite, four bundles, a rope, robe of material resembling animal skin.

Setting: A bare stage. There is a Chinese-type picture of a snow-capped mountain hanging from a bamboo frame on upstage center wall. At left there is a door marked "Entrance," and at right a door marked "Exit."

Lighting: No special effects.

Robin Hood and the Match at Nottingham

Characters: 8 male; 2 female; any number of male and female extras for courtiers, ladies-in-waiting, and townspeople.

Playing Time: 20 minutes.

Costumes: Traditional dress of medieval England. Robin Hood and his men wear ragged clothes; the Prince, Queen, Courtiers, and Ladies-in-Waiting are elaborately clothed. The townspeople wear simple costumes typical of the period.

Properties: Bows, one gold-colored arrow, coins, note with message, autoharp (for lyre). For reasons of safety, it is suggested that real arrows not be used in the shooting scene.

Setting: The fair at Nottingham. At stage right are two rows of benches for courtiers and ladies-in-waiting, and for some of the townspeople. Upstage center is a raised platform decorated with ribbons, colored bunting, and flowers. It is from this platform that the archers pretend to shoot at the target off-stage left. Downstage left the side of a brightly colored tent may be seen.

Lighting: No special effects.

Music: Any English ballad tune may be used for Allan-a-Dale's song, or a traditional Robin Hood song may be sung. An autoharp is a good substitute for the lyre.

The French Cabinetmaker

Characters: 3 male; 5 female.

Playing Time: 20 minutes.

Costumes: Traditional French, but in grotesque clown styles.

Properties: Broken chair, saw, hammer, tools, checkered tablecloth, and a doorknob.

Setting: The cabinetmaker's workshop. Upstage center is a worktable, on which tools, etc., are placed. On the backstage wall is a large window, and there are doors downstage left and right. Furniture, in various stages of repair, is placed about the room.

Lighting: No special effects.

THE GATES OF DINKELSBUEHL

Characters: 7 male; 1 female; as many male and female extras for the Children's Band as desired.

Playing Time: 25 minutes.

Costumes: Traditional Swedish and German.

Properties: Musical instruments for Children's Band; letter for the messenger; swords for the Swedish soldiers.

Setting: The main street of Dinkelsbuehl. There are high gates upstage center which form a wall across the back of the stage. The right and left walls of the stage may represent a street scene, with houses, shop entrances, etc. A street runs from left to right, and the main street, leading from the gates, meets it upstage center.

Lighting: No special effects.

Music: Any American square dance may be used for the Swedish folk dance.

THE SKILL OF PERICLES

Characters: 7 male; 3 female; as many male and female as desired to be citizens of Athens.

Playing Time: 25 minutes.

Costumes: The traditional classical Greek costumes. Pericles wears a ragged cloak with a hood over his costume.

Properties: Brass gong and scroll for Messenger, wooden sword for Ajax.

Setting: The market place in Athens. The backdrop shows the front of a Greek building with steps leading up to it. At left and right are stalls in which the merchants sell fruit, animals, pottery and other wares.

Lighting: No special effects.

Music: Bach's "A Song of Praise" may be found on page 76 of "New Music Horizons" (Book 2), published by Silver, Burdett Co., 1948. In place of this, any traditional Greek song may be used, such as "The Sponge Diver," page 170 in *Music In Our Country*, Book Five, Silver Burdett Co., 1957.

A LEAK IN THE DIKE

Characters: 4 male; 4 female.

Playing Time: 15 minutes.

Costumes: Traditional Dutch.

Properties: Book, for Jan; basket covered with a white napkin, for Netty; blanket and ointment, for Borein Apeldoorn; wooden tool box, for Haas; covered jug and piece of kuchen (coffee cake) for Netty's second entrance.

Setting: The rear wall of the stage represents the dike, extending the height and length of the stage. Along the base are tulips, made of construction paper.

Lighting: Lights dim and brighten as indicated in the text. A single spotlight should shine on Jan in the second scene.

OUR SISTER, SITYA

Characters: 6 male; 2 female.

Playing Time: 10 minutes.

Costumes: The dress of the characters indicates who they are. Dalang, Rama, and Ardjuna, the good male characters, are dressed in brocade silk trousers and a bold-patterned batik print waistcloth from which two silk scarves drape to the floor. A golden headdress, bracelets and jewelled earrings complete the costume. The evil characters. Sedyo and Rahajoe, wear heavy mats of black hair all over their bodies. Their make-up should emphasize bulging eyes, red faces, beards, and even fangs. Sitya and Jittith wear brown and white batik skirts and black velvet bodices. Their arms are bare. Their hair, worn loosely, is crowned with gold headdresses. Paku wears a white robe, and his make-up is red and white.

Properties: Gold-braided noose for Paku.

Setting: The stage represents the throne room of Ardjuna. At upstage center is the throne chair. Downstage left is a pallet, on which the king and queen are sitting at rise.

Lighting: No special effects.

THE COURTERS

Characters: 5 male; 1 female. The part of Brighella may be taken by a girl if another female role is desired.

Playing Time: 25 minutes.

Costumes: Flavio and Isabella wear typical costumes of the sixteenth century. The other characters are dressed to get as many laughs as possible; there are no restrictions and their costumes may be imaginative and colorful. Dottore and Pantalone later appear dressed as women with wigs, long full skirts, etc.

Properties: Large book and quill pen for Dottore.

Setting: A city square of an Italian town in the sixteenth century. There are no properties on stage, but a painted backdrop of a city square scene is across the rear of the stage. If desired a water fountain may be placed upstage center.

Lighting: No special effects.

BOSHIBARI AND THE TWO THIEVES

Characters: 3 male, or 1 male and 2 female.

Playing Time: 12 minutes.

Costumes: Medieval Japanese—ornate for the master and simple and identical for the servants. The make-up should be bold (reds, whites, and blacks) and stylized (circles for cheeks, triangles for shadows beneath the eyes).

Properties: Two long poles, four loops of rope, two signs, a tree, apples.

Setting: The scenes are representative, rather than realistic. For the house scene, a sign, reading, "The House of Daimyo." The orchard scene has a single stylized tree with apples hanging from strings stiffly arranged on it, and a sign, "The Orchard of Daimyo."

Lighting: No special effects.

Note: The movements of the characters should be precise, and the lines should be spoken with calmness and seriousness.

Licha's Birthday Serenade

Characters: 6 male; 8 female. As many or as few serenaders as desired may be used, but they should be kept in couples.

Playing Time: 20 minutes.

Costumes: Traditional Mexican. Pablo wears blue jeans, white shirt, wide-brimmed straw hat, and huaraches (sandals). Mama wears a long skirt, dark blouse, bright shawl, and huaraches. Luisa and Señor and Señora Hidalgo wear city clothes with a Mexican appearance. Boy serenaders wear dark trousers, white shirts, red flowing ties and waist sashes, sombreros, and black shoes. Girl serenaders and Licha wear colorful, flowing skirts and blouses, and flowers in their hair, and huaraches.

Properties: Head masks of a funny, male face for all serenaders. Masks may be made of white cloth with the features of the face painted in bright colors, or regular Halloween masks may be used. Guitars, violins, and trumpets for boy serenaders. Bracelet for Luisa. A gold foil circle attached to a pole to represent the sun, and a silver foil crescent attached to a pole to represent the moon.

Setting: The yard in front of Licha's house. Upstage center the front of a little adobe hut is seen: a solid wall with an opening for a door, and a pitched roof, covered with straw. Downstage, left and right, framing the house but not blocking the view, are two stone walls about two feet high, made by piling flat stones on top of each other.

Lighting: A spot may be used on the sun and moon at the beginning and end of the play, if desired.

The Golden Voice of Little Erik

Characters: 6 male; 3 female; male and female extras for townspeople.

Playing Time: 15 minutes.

Costumes: Little Erik and the three beggars are dressed in rags. The old beggar woman wears a shawl over her head; the man wears a woolen scarf, and the little girl wears men's shoes that are too big. The sheriff and the merchant wear rich robes and hats with plumes. Christina and the townspeople are dressed in peasant costume.

Properties: Broom, for Erik; purse

with three large pennies (British coins are the right size), for sheriff; staff, for second beggar; sack containing a plumed hat, silk blouse, trousers and a cloak, for merchant.

Setting: The stage represents a street. The backdrop is a jail, which may be sketched in charcoal. There is a bench in front of the jail.

Lighting: No special effects.

Music: The words are to the tune of "The Norwegian Dance #2" by Edvard Grieg.

STANISLAW AND THE WOLF

Characters: 6 male; 3 female.

Playing Time: 15 minutes.

Costumes: Stanislaw has white hair and beard. He wears animal skins. The little boy, old woman, and blacksmith are appropriately dressed. The blacksmith wears a black apron. The animals may wear simple or elaborate costumes, as desired.

Properties: Earthen bowl and flat stone, for Stanislaw; books strapped together, for Roddey; market basket, for Bertha; large club, for Walter (this should be made of cardboard, so that it can be swung freely and with a great deal of noise); large white napkin, for Adolph.

Setting: A clearing in the woods, in front of the hut of St. Stanislaw. Upstage center is the outline of the hut, with a door leading offstage rear. Surrounding the hut are trees and bushes. A large club is hidden in the bushes.

Lighting: No special effects.

THE HIGHLAND FLING

Characters: 4 male; 4 female; male and female extras.

Playing Time: 25 minutes.

Costumes: Traditional Scotch. The men wear plaid kilts and scarfs, white blouses, caps, calf-length socks, and shoes. The women wear velvet jackets over their blouses, and tams instead of caps. Mary has a shawl over her head. (See *Dramatic Costumes for Children* by Edith Dabney and C. M. Wise, Educational Publishers, 1949.)

Properties: Pipe for Garty.

Setting: The open country of Scotland. At center is a rude, plank bridge, with rails upstage and downstage. At right and left of the bridge are two huge boulders (or clumps of bushes). These are large enough to conceal each of the clans from the audience. The backdrop is of hills and sky.

Lighting: No special effects.

Music: There are a number of tunes used with these lyrics and any tune that fits the occasion may be used. Music for all the songs may be found in *Scotland in Song* (Remick Music Corp., New York, 1957), and in most standard collections of folk songs.

THE MAGIC OF SALAMANCA

Characters: 4 male; 2 female.

Playing Time: 20-25 minutes.

Costumes: Traditional Spanish costumes; Pancracio wears elegant clothes of a wealthy man.

Properties: Guitar, laundry basket, broom, bread, fruit, cheese, suitcase.

Setting: A road. There is a house upstage center, with an open window next to the door. The window is covered with a curtain that can be pushed aside. Downstage left of the house is a small bin (packing box), and a small door leading into the bin.

Lighting: No special effects.

Music: "Vagabond Song" may be found on page 57 of *Singing America* (C. C. Birchard, Boston). Any traditional Spanish folk song may be used in its place.

THE SON OF WILLIAM TELL

Characters: 8 male; 3 female.

Playing Time: 20 minutes.

Costumes: All of the characters wear simple Swiss Alpine clothing, except Gessler and Friesshardt, who may wear ornate uniforms. The boys wear hats.

Properties: Five bows for William, Tell, and the mountaineers, arrows with rubber tips, apple for Hildegarde, sword for Friesshardt.

Setting: An open meadow. Several rocks and bushes may be placed around the stage. The backdrop should depict the mountains.

Lighting: No special effects.

JOHNNY APPLESEED

Characters: 6 male; 3 female.

Playing Time: 20 minutes.

Costumes: Traditional frontier, except for Johnny Appleseed, who is wearing a pair of ragged trousers, a flour sack for a shirt, a saucepan for a hat. A rope is tied around his waist and attached to it is a green pouch in which he has a Bible. He carries a sack with appleseeds over his shoulder.

Properties: Bible, sack with apple seeds, sawhorse, guns for the outlaws.

Setting: A clearing in the woods. Upstage center is the entrance to the Fogles' log cabin. Downstage right, the back of the Fogles' wagon may be seen. Downstage center is a pile of logs.

Lighting: No special effects.